_____

TO

_____

FROM

_____

DATE

Sacred Rest

Finding the Sabbath
in the Everyday

Cheryl Wunderlich

THOMAS NELSON
Since 1798

Published in Nashville, Tennessee, by Thomas Nelson. Thomas Nelson is a registered trademark of HarperCollins Christian Publishing, Inc.

Unless otherwise noted, Scripture quotations are taken from Scripture quotations marked NIV are taken from the Holy Bible, New International Version®, NIV®. Copyright © 1973, 1978, 1984, 2011 by Biblica, Inc.™ Used by permission of Zondervan. All rights reserved worldwide. www.zondervan.com. The "NIV" and "New International Version" are trademarks registered in the United States Patent and Trademark Office by Biblica, Inc.®

Scripture quotations marked ESV are taken from the ESV® Bible (The Holy Bible, English Standard Version®), copyright © 2001 by Crossway, a publishing ministry of Good News Publishers. Used by permission. All rights reserved.

Scripture quotations marked NASB are taken from the New American Standard Bible®, Copyright © 1960, 1962, 1963, 1968, 1971, 1972, 1973, 1975, 1977, 1995 by The Lockman Foundation. Used by permission. (www.Lockman.org)

Scripture quotations marked NKJV are taken from the New King James Version®. © 1982 by Thomas Nelson. Used by permission. All rights reserved.

Scripture quotations marked NLT are taken from the Holy Bible, New Living Translation. © 1996, 2004, 2007, 2013, 2015 by Tyndale House Foundation. Used by permission of Tyndale House Publishers, Inc., Carol Stream, Illinois 60188. All rights reserved.

Scripture quotations marked WEB are taken from the World English Bible™. Public domain.

All italics in Scripture quotations are added by the author.

ISBN-13: 978-0-7180-9733-2

Printed in China

18 19 20 21 22 GRI 6 5 4 3 2

INTRODUCTION

I never realized resting could be so difficult—until I was diagnosed with breast cancer. I was forty-two years old. My sprint through life as a mother of three active children came to a screeching halt. Surgery and chemotherapy meant stepping down from my role as director of women's ministries at a large church and retreating from the activities that made me feel significant. If that wasn't difficult enough, another cancer diagnosis five years later abruptly interrupted my life. Cancer had forced me to rest against my will, and I resented it.

Resting felt like being trapped under a one-ton boulder. My long days seemed pointless because I wasn't accomplishing anything. And if I could manage to rest physically, I couldn't calm the anxious thoughts swirling through my mind.

Sensing my struggle, an older woman from church reached out. She told me that knowing God *just to know Him* was a worthier endeavor than anything else. She told me I had to make resting the most important, nonnegotiable activity each day. She reassured me I could trust God to use those around me to accomplish everything else. I left that precious conversation determined to rest. I learned quickly, however, that resting is easier said than done.

Why do we struggle with rest? We long for an afternoon at the beach or stolen hour to read a book. But often these mini-breaks never come. We are experts at pushing ourselves beyond healthy limits. Social media and smartphones reinforce this frenetic lifestyle. We pride ourselves on accomplishments, even more if they include good things like ministry. Inside, though, we grow emptier and emptier. I never realized how empty I had become until my unwelcome season of rest.

At a loss, I turned to the Bible and began a quest to examine every verse that mentioned *rest*. My findings astounded me. How had I gotten so far off course? And as I looked at the harried lives of others, I realized that most of us are off course.

I had spent my entire life *doing* things for God but had missed *knowing* Him intimately because my life was void of rest. That's what busyness does. It sweeps us up into its current and carries us downstream, away from God. He calls from the riverbank to swim ashore and rest with Him. Often we're so far away that His voice is barely audible above the roar. We exhaust ourselves trying to stay afloat and call to Him only when we're desperate.

I hope this devotional will be a lifeline to pull you from the clutches of our busy world. I pray you'll refocus, quiet your weary soul, and experience the refreshment of connecting with God. Rest is important to God. He set aside an entire day of creation for rest. In fact, the Hebrew word for *rest* the first time it appears in the Bible is the same as our word *Sabbath*, which means to stop all labor. God knew rest would be essential to our spiritual, physical, and emotional well-being; it's not just a nice added extra. Sabbath rest is a gift from God. Take time to savor the quiet moments He has planned for you to come away from our busy world and draw near to Him.

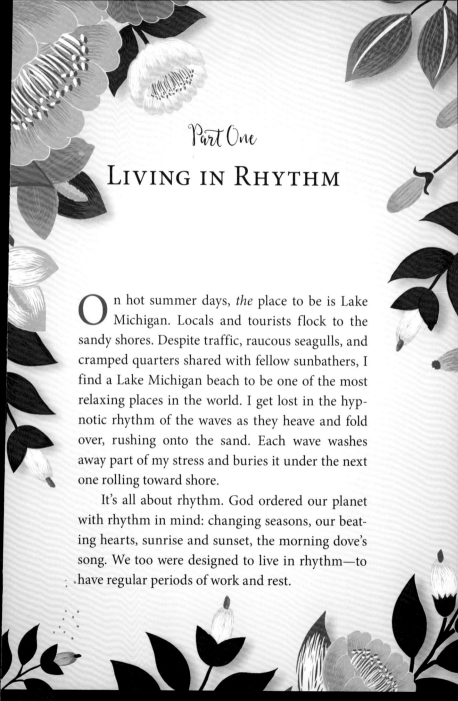

Part One

LIVING IN RHYTHM

On hot summer days, *the* place to be is Lake Michigan. Locals and tourists flock to the sandy shores. Despite traffic, raucous seagulls, and cramped quarters shared with fellow sunbathers, I find a Lake Michigan beach to be one of the most relaxing places in the world. I get lost in the hypnotic rhythm of the waves as they heave and fold over, rushing onto the sand. Each wave washes away part of my stress and buries it under the next one rolling toward shore.

It's all about rhythm. God ordered our planet with rhythm in mind: changing seasons, our beating hearts, sunrise and sunset, the morning dove's song. We too were designed to live in rhythm—to have regular periods of work and rest.

One

CREATED FOR REST

Thus the heavens and the earth were completed
in all their vast array. By the seventh day God
had finished the work he had been doing; so on
the seventh day he rested from all his work.
—GENESIS 2:1–2

After creating day, night, sky, seas, land, vegetation, sun, moon, stars, creatures, men, and women—all we know and see in the universe—God rested. As the all-powerful God of the universe, He was not tired after all that hard work. He simply spoke, and by the power of His word, creation instantaneously happened! He could have spoken the entire universe into existence with one command, but He didn't. Could He have been trying to teach us something?

God followed an orderly process in His creative activity. At the beginning of each day, God proclaimed, "Let there be . . ." and the book of Genesis tells us "it was so." Each of God's workdays concluded the same way: "And there was evening and there was morning." This pattern repeated without variation throughout creation week until the seventh day, when God stopped working with a grand pause, creating a full day of rest in the absence of any work.

You can hear a cadence as the Creator works. There's a built-in rhythm of work followed by rest. He worked six days with an evening break between each and rested for a full day at the end. God didn't pull any all-nighters—even though He had the whole universe to create. He was giving us a gift on top of the spectacular creation He made from nothing: He was giving us permission to take a break and rest. In fact, He designed all of creation to operate in a rhythm of work and rest just as He does. You, and all of creation, were never intended to operate around the clock. Your loving God designed you to stop all work and rest on a regular basis.

Lord, how far my life falls short of Your grand design. How has rest become so rare in my personal world and in the world around me? Lord, reawaken the restful rhythms You instilled in me at creation. Rescue me from self-imposed busyness, and teach me to live Your way.

3

Two

OFF THE HAMSTER WHEEL

God blessed the seventh day and made it holy, because on
it he rested from all the work of creating that he had done.
—GENESIS 2:3

D o you ever feel like a hamster running on an exercise wheel, going and going but not really getting anywhere? With e-mail, texting, smartphones, laptops, and the Internet, we can work around the clock. Many of us try to keep this wheel going, promising ourselves that next week won't be so busy or we'll catch up on our sleep over the weekend. But we never do. This hamster-wheel existence is not as harmless as we think.

It tempts us to start cutting out things we think can wait—relationships with family and friends, time with God or exercise, healthy eating, and sleep—for the sake of accomplishing a few more things. As a result, we start to feel empty, physically run-down, and far from God.

How can we reconcile these crazy lives with God's perfectly beautiful design, which incorporates regular rest? God values rest so much that He dedicated an entire day, the Sabbath, to doing nothing at all. God sets this day apart as holy. He does not consider it a waste of time or a luxury. Otherwise why would God dedicate one day in His seven-day creation week for all work to stop—a day to be honored and devoted to Him?

As our Creator, God gets how our minds work. He understands the temptation to get so wrapped up in the pressures and demands of daily living that we forget He created us for Him, that we belong to Him. Rest is the antidote to that forgetfulness. God knew that without rest we would get sucked into the culture around us and start living for ourselves. So instead of pushing Him to the backs of our minds, let's take a rest. Let's get off that wheel and stop to remember who is really in charge. It's the God who made us, enjoys our company, and gives us peace.

Lord, sometimes rest seems like a luxury I can't afford. But I'm so glad that's not really the case. Help me to value rest as much as You do so I will stop more often to be with You. That way I can reflect the peace and joy of knowing You to a lost world without being as stressed-out as everyone else! Show me how to step off the wheel today.

Three

BALANCING ACT

"Six days you shall labor and do all your work,
but the seventh day is a sabbath to the LORD
your God. On it you shall not do any work."
—EXODUS 20:9–10

I remember playing hopscotch with my sisters when I was growing up. When we were bored, we'd scrounge around in the garage for a piece of chalk, draw a grid on the driveway, and number it from one to ten. We would toss a stone on each square in sequence and hop on one leg and then two, skipping over the square with the stone. The tricky part was keeping our balance, especially when trying to skip over the square with the stone. I would breathe a small sigh of relief when I reached square ten, the rest stop, where I could catch my balance and turn around for the trip back to start.

Keeping God's commandment to rest can be a lot like playing hopscotch. We often try to skip it without losing our balance, but it's very hard to do! Rest is one of the Ten Commandments, right up there with "Do not murder" and "Do not steal." Although we wouldn't consider murdering, stealing, or violating the other commandments, we don't seem to have a problem skipping His command to rest. Why is that? Maybe we feel guilty for resting because we view it as lazy or unproductive—especially if we are doing godly things such as serving at church or helping the poor. But what if rest is more than a break for us? What if it's a bigger statement?

When God commanded the Israelites to do no work on the Sabbath, He had a greater purpose. He wasn't just giving them another rule to follow. A day of rest was to be a sign—a distinguishing mark that set God's people apart from all the nations around them. In the same way, Christians are meant to live at a different pace from the restless culture around us. It's a sign to a lost world that we belong to God.

God knows that when we try to skip rest, it will throw us off balance. Without rest, we can fall into the trap of living for ourselves and for all we can achieve. But we couldn't achieve a single thing without Him! So let's take a moment to rest and rebalance. To slow down and be radically different, showing the world by example that there's something and Someone better to live for!

> *Lord, I can get so focused on everything I need to do that I skip setting aside time to spend with You. Please reorder my priorities and help me give myself permission to receive Your promised rest, trusting You to provide when I'm not working. Then I will be able to rest in something bigger and greater than all my accomplishments—You.*

Four

THE FALLOW FIELD

"For six years sow your fields, and for six years prune your vineyards and gather their crops. But in the seventh year the land is to have a year of sabbath rest, a sabbath to the LORD. . . . I will send you such a blessing in the sixth year that the land will yield enough for three years."
—LEVITICUS 25:3–4, 21

I magine you're driving through the countryside in springtime, and you spot an empty field missing the fresh green shoots of the surrounding farmland. It may look like a waste of space, but the fallow field reflects how God designed the earth to operate. Farmers need to rest their land. If they plant the same crop too many years in a row in the same field, the land will not yield a profitable harvest. The same principle applies to nature: seasons change and trees shed their leaves in a blazing fall display to make way for a dormant period during winter. Look and see a rhythm of work and rest designed by God.

God takes care of the trees as they lie dormant until He reawakens them in the spring. He replenishes nutrients in fallow soil. When we rest, He will provide for us too. It takes great faith to rest. Resting means that some things will be left undone. That's a challenge of rest: believing that everything will not fall apart if we step away from our responsibilities and stop trying to hold everything together. Remember, our God holds all creation together, and He can do it without our help!

He promises over and over in the Bible that He will take care of our needs. Refresh your heart with these truths: "God is able to bless you abundantly, so that in all things at all times, having all that you need, you will abound in every good work" (2 Corinthians 9:8). He made the universe and owns all the resources within it. His treasury is full of blessings He is waiting to pour out on His children. We can rest assured that just as He provides the strength for us to work, He will provide all we need when we rest.

Lord, as long as I continue to think it's up to me to hold things together, I will never rest. All I need is to look out my window for evidence of Your tender and personal care. Just as You take care of creation, You take care of me whether I'm working or doing nothing at all.

Five

SACRED ASSEMBLIES

*"On the first day hold a sacred assembly and do
no regular work. For seven days present a food
offering to the* LORD. *And on the seventh day hold
a sacred assembly and do no regular work."*
—LEVITICUS 23:7–8

How good are you at multitasking? Can you carry on a conversation while making dinner and answering text messages? You might think you're accomplishing several things at once, but research has revealed something surprising. Scientists say our brains are not wired to focus on more than one task at a time. In reality, our multitasking brains are switching quickly back and forth between separate activities. And in the long run, researchers say, performance suffers and energy is depleted. This means multitaskers actually accomplish less than one-task-at-a-time workers. Something, or someone, always gets the short end of the stick.

God told His followers about this generations before all our scientific research. When He handed down the first set of laws for His people more than two thousand years ago, He made it clear that they were not to multitask or do any work during the Israelites' festivals and special worship days (sacred assemblies).

Why? The only way we'll develop a relationship with God and get to know Him better is by spending time with Him. The same goes for our relationships with others in the church—our very own sacred assembly. God designed us to operate in community, where we share our burdens, our resources, our prayers, and our lives. In the early church, "every day they continued to meet together in the temple courts. They broke bread in their homes and ate together with glad and sincere hearts, praising God and enjoying the favor of all the people" (Acts 2:46–47). What a beautiful way to live!

Chronic busyness, like multitasking, does more than exhaust us: it weakens our relationships, weakens the church, and makes worship all but impossible. Today try focusing on one thing at a time. Be present and enjoy a singular focus on each activity, each person, and each moment that the Father gives you.

Lord, I never want to run through life so quickly that I fail to see the needs of my loved ones or those in my community. Show me how to do one thing at a time and foster closeness in the church family, of which You have made me an indispensable part. I don't want to miss out anymore.

11

Six

SURVIVE AND THRIVE

"The Sabbath was made for man, not man for the Sabbath."
—MARK 2:27

My son's friend stopped by the other day. As we were standing around the kitchen talking, I asked him how he and his siblings were surviving with his mom and dad away on a six-week missions trip. He smiled and said, "We're doing more than surviving. We're thriving!" That was not the answer I expected! He explained that he liked being able to do as he pleased without anyone telling him what to do, such as pick up his pants from the couch. I chuckled to myself. We all like being able to do whatever we want without constraints.

I know his parents well, and they don't run their home like a boot camp. Though it might feel freeing to leave your pants on the couch and not have to pick them up, it wouldn't be so fun to go into your closet two weeks later and find no clean pants to wear. Nor would it be nice to have no space on the couch to plop down and relax when you came home. Mom and Dad have the big picture in mind and know that their kids need clean clothes and a warm, orderly, and inviting environment to regroup after a long day. That's why they have rules—because they love their children and want to do what's best for them.

Our heavenly Father is the same way. He loves us and wants to provide what's best for us—even though we'd often rather do what we want. God gives the gift of Sabbath rest as a blessing, not another burdensome rule to keep. God knows that, if left to ourselves, we'll keep running and never stop. Our world is filled with so many fascinating things to do and try and enjoy—and responsibilities to fulfill and work to do. Our natural inclination is to plow full-steam ahead. Yet God already knows how that will end if we don't take a break.

God intended a day of rest to be a boundary to keep us from working ourselves into the ground. A day of rest is far from being a restriction. God sees the big picture and does not want us to miss out on the beautiful gifts He desires to give us when we rest, such as calm assurance, peaceful hearts, and renewed strength to tackle another day. Our loving Father does not just want us to survive; He wants us to thrive.

Lord, even though I am all grown up, I still need to learn how to go to my room and have a quiet time. I haven't always liked it, but I see the great wisdom behind it now—it helps me thrive. Help me to accept rest as a loving gift You give because You want to take care of me. You know best.

13

Seven

FOREVER REST

*"The people of Israel shall keep the Sabbath,
observing the Sabbath throughout their
generations, as a covenant forever."*
—EXODUS 31:16 ESV

*F*orever is a long time. *Forever* goes on without end. God instituted Sabbath rest as a "covenant forever" between Him and His chosen people, which means rest is to go beyond our days on Earth. Isn't that a comforting thought?

This idea of ceasing our everyday work to rest with God points to a greater day. When we pass from this life one day, we will be able to put down our work once and for all and breathe a sigh of relief—no more responsibilities, no more pressures, no more deadlines. At that point, if our faith is in Jesus, we will enter eternity and experience a new kind of rest. We will rest with God in heaven. When we declare faith in Jesus Christ, in His death and resurrection, He forgives our sins. He invites us to know Him both on this earth and face-to-face in heaven—forever.

On the unbelievably hard days, we can look forward to knowing that better days of heavenly rest lay ahead. As a three-time cancer survivor, I have often wished I were already there. God is good to use our struggles to increase our longing for our home in heaven. Yet while we wait for that incredible day to arrive, we all have important jobs God has given us. Let's not waste our time. As the apostle Paul said, "To me, to live is Christ and to die is gain. . . . I desire to depart and be with Christ, which is better by far; but it is more necessary for you that I remain in the body. Convinced of this, I know that I will remain, and I will continue with all of you for your progress and joy in the faith" (Philippians 1:21, 23–25).

Our lives are a dress rehearsal for that glorious day when we will see Him face-to-face. As we learn to rest with Him on this earth, and as we go about the purposes He has given us, we are preparing for eternity—our forever rest with God.

Lord, help me not to lose sight of forever. I want to be ready for eternity. Teach me how to pull away from the busyness of life and rest in Your presence. After all, I'm going to spend much more time with You in heaven than I will on Earth.

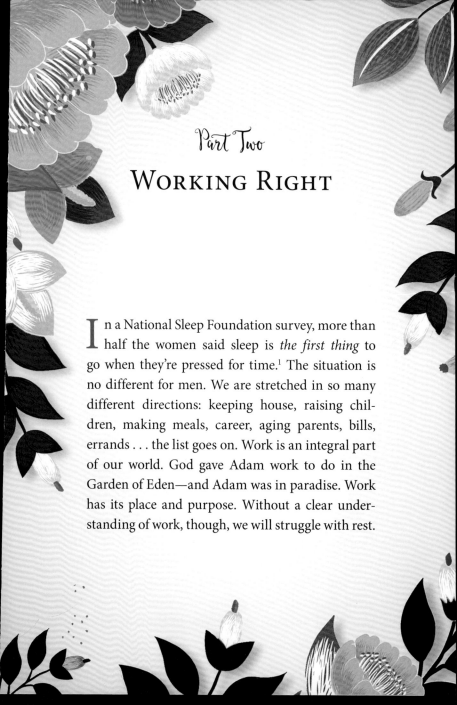

Part Two

WORKING RIGHT

In a National Sleep Foundation survey, more than half the women said sleep is *the first thing* to go when they're pressed for time.[1] The situation is no different for men. We are stretched in so many different directions: keeping house, raising children, making meals, career, aging parents, bills, errands . . . the list goes on. Work is an integral part of our world. God gave Adam work to do in the Garden of Eden—and Adam was in paradise. Work has its place and purpose. Without a clear understanding of work, though, we will struggle with rest.

Eight

GOOD WORK

The LORD God took the man and put him in the
Garden of Eden to work it and take care of it.
—GENESIS 2:15

After creating Adam and breathing life into him, God gave him a job. He brought him to a perfect paradise, the Garden of Eden, and put him to work caring for it. Adam's cultivating work was to be done in service to God. By entrusting Adam with this responsibility, God also gave him authority to carry out the work. God placed His treasured garden in Adam's hands to watch over and protect as he saw fit. The task was designed for Adam's enjoyment and satisfaction as he saw the fruit of his labor in a well-tended garden.

God gives each of us work too. We're each tending a garden, and we each have fruit to produce. Our work might be a job we do for a paycheck or responsibilities such as caring for a home, raising a family, or serving at church or in the community. Whatever our work, God wants us to find fulfillment and satisfaction as we use the skills and gifts He has given us. Just as with Adam, God wants us to see our work first and foremost as a service to Him. As Solomon said, "I know that there is nothing better for people than to be happy and to do good while they live. That each of them may eat and drink, and find satisfaction in all their toil—this is the gift of God" (Ecclesiastes 3:12–13).

Work is God's gift to us. Work is an opportunity to use our intellect, resources, physical strength, and creativity to do something useful, productive, and beautiful. God designed us to find satisfaction in our accomplishments. We must beware of falling into the trap of working for work's sake instead of as service to God. Work can become tedious and futile if we don't see God's grander intention behind it. Once we see that and work well, then we can rest well.

Lord, work is Your gift to me. Help me to remember that I am ultimately serving You in every task I do. Then my work will always be worthwhile.

19

Nine

ROCKY GROUND

To Adam he said, "Because you listened to your wife and ate fruit from the tree about which I commanded you, 'You must not eat from it,' cursed is the ground because of you; through painful toil you will eat from it all the days of your life."
—GENESIS 3:17

D o you ever get exasperated when you scrub the kitchen floor, then the dog comes in and drags mud all over it? Or you spend two hours edging and mowing the lawn only to wake up the next day and discover that a mole has tunneled across the front yard? Or what about working into the wee hours of the morning to produce a stellar presentation, only to find out your boss will handle it instead? If work seems frustrating or even futile at times, you can blame Adam and Eve.

Everything changed the moment they ate from the tree of the knowledge of good and evil, which the Lord had explicitly forbidden. As a result of their disobedience, God cursed the ground and the work they had to do, and He drove them from perfect paradise into a fallen world. The work Adam did in the garden now would be difficult and unproductive. He would labor long and hard to provide for his family. Just as Adam and Eve rebelled against God, so the world where they lived and worked would rebel against them.

When you're struggling with work and feel unable to fully rest, know there is a good explanation: *Work itself is not part of the curse. Unproductive, backbreaking work is the curse.* Ultimately that's why we struggle with a tension between work and rest. Work, which God intended to bring joy and satisfaction, is marred by pain and hardship. Simple tasks become time-consuming, and more and more effort is required to reach a goal. Yet God, in His love for us, does not leave us to struggle alone. He provides strength when we call on Him for help and gives us grace to overcome sin.

The problem started with sin, "but thanks be to God! He gives us the victory through our Lord Jesus Christ. Therefore . . . stand firm. Let nothing move you. Always give yourselves fully to the work of the Lord, because you know that your labor in the Lord is not in vain" (1 Corinthians 15:57–58). What a promise! We can rest assured that the Lord can give us power to be victorious in our endeavors despite the toil required to be productive in our fallen world. We need never despair because He is with us.

Lord, only You can provide the power to overcome sin. When I call upon You, You provide grace and strength to do the work You have given me.

Ten

SLEEPING AND WAKING

In vain you rise early and stay up late, toiling for food to eat—for he grants sleep to those he loves.
—PSALM 127:2

When I told my son it was time to put on his shoes, I thought it was so cute the first time he proudly said, "I do it self." *How wonderful!* I thought. *He's becoming independent.* But it wasn't so cute the tenth time. I soon realized that "I do it self" meant watching a long struggle for those inexperienced little fingers to tug on socks, pull on a shirt, or wrestle with shoes that inevitably ended up on the wrong feet. How much easier it would have been for both of us if he would accept my help, especially when I was in a hurry.

I wonder if our heavenly Father might feel the same way when we assert our independence by giving Him the grown-up version of "I do it self." Often we see ourselves as the center of our work universe. We think our success relies on our own efforts, so we drive ourselves into the ground, believing everything will fall apart if we don't keep tight control. But this line of thinking leaves God out of the center of the work equation—and He is the One who makes work worthwhile.

The Bible tells us that getting up early and staying up

late consistently to get all our work done is vain—useless, futile, worthless, pointless. That's the fundamental difference between *work* and *toil*, which is labor marked by pain and hardship. Many of us know the pain of exhausting ourselves day after day, sacrificing sleep and our physical, mental, and emotional well-being to keep up with work. Could it be because we're trying to do it all ourselves instead of allowing the God of the universe to be in charge?

We don't have to operate this way. Why? The psalmist tells us God "grants sleep to those he loves." When we sleep, we lie down and let go. God sustains our breathing, reenergizes our bodies, and keeps the universe running until we wake. Being in a state of sleeping rest is a beautiful picture of trusting in God's perfect care. He wants us to truly rest—to give up control of all we must accomplish each day and put the outcome in His hands, resting in the fact that He will help us do what is needed and give us the wisdom to know what we should let go.

> *God, I don't want to struggle for control and toil away painfully when I could know Your peace. Help me to surrender and let You help me in all my work; it always turns out better when I do. Show me which things to put down. You hold my future firmly in Your hands.*

Eleven

TRUE RENEWAL

Those who hope in the LORD will renew their strength.
They will soar on wings like eagles; they will run and
not grow weary, they will walk and not be faint.
—ISAIAH 40:31

"Work hard, play hard" is a common motto in our day. Our culture is marked by extremes. On one hand, we can drive ourselves to work fourteen-hour days, and on the other hand, we can burn hours on Facebook, the latest computer game, or sitting in front of the TV in an attempt to escape the stress. Our souls seek renewal after being depleted, but often we are too exhausted to engage in activities that truly refresh.

Strangely enough, escaping into our own media-made world can have the same effect as being too busy. Without realizing it, we can use the noise to replace work frenzy and end up drowning out the still, small voice of God, who provides our only true source of renewal (not to mention isolating ourselves from life-giving relationships with others). We long to soar on wings like eagles but end up on a great escape instead!

Yes, being able to do absolutely nothing seems like paradise, and it certainly can be for the bone-weary soul. But have you ever noticed that the more time you take off, the more you sit around and fritter away the day, the harder it is when it's time to go back to work? Anyone who has ever procrastinated knows the guilt and hopelessness that come as the work piles up until it seems impossible to conquer. The compounded problems of working too little can be as hard to bear as working too much.

So let's stop going from one extreme to the other—pushing beyond our limits, collapsing in front of the TV, and having to return, exhausted, to the stresses we left behind. God wants to be our true source of renewal. Time with Him, instead of the world's draining idea of rest or avoidance, will recharge us and reframe our lives. Our loving God stands ready to infuse our weary souls with new strength. He is only a prayer away.

Lord, help me to reach for Your Word instead of for the TV remote or the computer. Life always seems more manageable after I've spent time with You.

Twelve

WORKS OF ART

We are God's handiwork, created in Christ Jesus to do
good works, which God prepared in advance for us to do.
—EPHESIANS 2:10

I often see God, our magnificent Creator, as an artist. Imagine Him bent over a pottery wheel, skillful hands molding a lump of clay into a one-of-a-kind masterpiece. He sees in His mind's eye what He wants to make before He begins. He might make a vase to display a spring bouquet, a mug that, when filled with coffee, will take the chill out of a cold morning, or a platter to grace a holiday table. He knows how to make each piece just right for the job.

Before the great Artist created each of us, He had a purpose in mind. As an artist chooses a unique color scheme, materials, and design for each creation, God chose the perfect combination of characteristics to make you well suited to perform the work He created you to do.

Some people were created to be Olympic athletes; some might have the brainpower to find a cure for cancer; some might be savvy enough to score big on Wall Street or become the CEO of a company. Some might forego a career to stay home and raise their children; some might be committed to behind-the-scenes work serving others; some might be jacks-of-all-trades with broad accomplishments in many areas. No matter what we do—whether we are in the spotlight trying to accomplish something great or diligently doing the tasks in front of us—only what we do for God will last beyond our lives on Earth.

Sometimes we wonder, *Is what I'm doing worth it? Am I doing what I'm* supposed *to do?* We can waste a great deal of precious energy questioning whether we're doing God's will rather than moving ahead freely with the work He's given us. But there's no need to fret. You can rest confidently in God's sovereign guidance. Just as He created you with a unique set of gifts and skills, He also will bring you hand-tailored opportunities to work and serve Him. The tasks He brings might not be the same as you see everyone else doing. They might not be easy. They might not even be your first choice. But your faithfulness is what matters in the end. Our Creator knows us even better than we know ourselves. We will never regret saying yes to what He wants us to do.

Lord, You are the Potter. Help me, as Your clay, to submit to the gentle pressure of Your hands so I will become a beautiful vessel useful for Your purposes.

27

Thirteen

THE POINT OF WORK

Whatever you do, work at it with all your heart, as working for the Lord, not for human masters, since you know that you will receive an inheritance from the Lord as a reward. It is the Lord Christ you are serving.
—COLOSSIANS 3:23–24

My daughter, who is taking an advanced math class, told us that the chances of winning the lottery are about one in fourteen million. She and her class had crunched the numbers. Although the exact odds depend on many factors, winning the jackpot in which you pick six numbers correctly from a pool of forty-nine numbers is nearly impossible. But that's not the way it is with God. We have an inheritance from Him, 100 percent guaranteed, which is far better than winning any lottery.

If we can keep our eyes on the prize, our fast-paced world of work will carry so much more meaning than being merely a monotonous cycle of waking, working, sleeping, and waking again. We are not working just to make a living, raise a family, fulfill our responsibilities, or get tasks done with a little bit of fun thrown in between. In *whatever* we do, we are ultimately serving Christ. And what could be more important than that?

This might be easier to see if you're a missionary, pastor, Bible study leader, or Sunday school teacher. But God makes no separation between sacred and secular endeavors. We can serve Him in all we do, from washing dishes to working on a spreadsheet to teaching Sunday school. We're not just going to work and completing a task for the here and now. We're not just trying to please a boss or to garner others' approval. No, we're looking forward to the day when we hear the Lord say, "Well done, good and faithful servant!" (Matthew 25:21).

When we lay our heads on the pillow at night, we can rest knowing that our reward is secure, no matter how the day went. Even on the hardest days, we can take special comfort in the knowledge that God has seen all our endeavors. If done for Him, our efforts will be rewarded—a heavenly reward that cannot be exhausted or spent like lottery winnings. Our reward is put in our heavenly bank account and will be waiting for us to withdraw when we meet our Savior one day.

Lord, I have no problem staying busy. But I often stumble when it comes to making sure that all I do is in service to You. Help me to pause before I get out of bed and commit my work to You so I can rest well at night, knowing I've sought Your will for my life and I will receive my reward from You.

Fourteen

CHOOSE WHAT IS BETTER

Martha opened her home to [Jesus]. She had a sister called Mary, who sat at the Lord's feet listening to what he said. But Martha was distracted by all the preparations that had to be made. . . . "Martha, Martha," the Lord answered, "you are worried and upset about many things, but a few things are needed—or indeed only one. Mary has chosen what is better, and it will not be taken away from her."

—LUKE 10:38–42

*C*ompany's coming! I was a newlywed and my husband had invited a colleague over for dinner. I kicked into high hospitality gear. I wanted everything to be *perfect.* That way I could showcase my new cooking skills and show off how I had turned our tiny apartment into a wonderful home. Imagine my husband's shock to find me deep-cleaning our bedroom closet as I hurried around getting everything in order. "Aren't you going a little overboard?" he asked. "Do you think he's going to check out the closet?"

I look back at that time now and laugh, although I was irritated with him then for not appreciating all my hard work.

Working at something with all our hearts can turn into obsessing if we're not careful. We have a name for that:

perfectionism. Perfectionism could have been Martha's middle name. She shows all the classic signs of crossing the line from reasonable effort to pursuing perfection—worry, distraction, exhaustion, and resentment of others who refuse to help reach unrealistic expectations. These are red flags to warn us when we are getting off course.

Notice how Jesus lovingly helped Martha see that there was a better way. If our relentless activity steals all our time so there's none left to spend with Jesus and our loved ones, that's a sure sign we need to set better boundaries. When we do, the door to rest opens so we can be more like Mary, who chose what was (and is) always right: spending time with Jesus.

My friend Sara Perry had a great acronym for *busy*: Being Under Satan's Yoke. The Enemy likes to keep us busy doing trivial things so we won't have time to do what's important, the work God has created us to do. *Nothing is more important than spending time with Jesus and knowing Him.* When we do, we experience refreshment, peace, and His transforming power to make us more like Him. Resting with Jesus also gives space for Jesus to show us where we've gotten off track and give us strength to head in a better direction.

Lord, it's so easy for me to go overboard instead of keeping things simple. When I get caught up in perfectionism, I'm grateful for Your gentle reminders that I need to reset my priorities.

Fifteen

THE WORK OF THE HEART

They asked him, "What must we do to do the works God requires?" Jesus answered, "The work of God is this: to believe in the one he has sent."
—JOHN 6:28–29

Our one hundred-pound Bernese mountain dog will do anything for a tiny piece of hot dog. Oakley will stand perfectly still, lie down and stay, and charge across a field to sit down right in front of me when I call—all for a miniscule bit of hot dog. We learned the secret of positive reinforcement for molding good behavior in puppy kindergarten. Thankfully, Oakley has been an easy student with a strong desire to please because it's very hard to force a one hundred-pound dog to do anything! (I know. I've tried!)

Most of us are wired like Oakley. We want to please. We work ourselves into the ground to please the boss and get that promotion at work. Our children work for good grades or hustle to score the game-winning goal to earn our applause. Even as adults, we can still feel a need to please our parents, hoping to gain their praise for the way we raise our children or spend our money. Much of the drive behind our work is to satisfy our quest for approval.

But the greatest work we will ever do isn't done with our hands; it's done with our hearts. God is our Audience of One, and no work is required to earn His approval. All He wants is for us to turn our hearts over to Him, the only One who can save us. He accepts us just as we are and gives us the gift of His spotless holiness in place of our sins.

When we're working for the Lord, we aren't working to get into heaven. Our works—even the good things we do—would never be enough to cover our sin. As a stain ruins a new shirt, the stain of sin taints everything we do. "For all have sinned and fall short of the glory of God" (Romans 3:23).

The only "work" we can do is to place our faith and trust in Jesus Christ, who has already done all the work required to gain our entrance into heaven. Jesus paid the death penalty for our sin by dying on the cross and rising again. Knowing this should give you permission to rest. The only thing you can do to earn His approval is hold out your hands and receive the gift of eternal life.

Lord, when You look at me, You see past all the externals and look straight into my heart. Thank You for loving me so much that You sent Jesus to die for me so my heart could be made new. I am grateful I can rest because I don't have to earn this beautiful new life from You.

33

Sixteen

REST TO RECOVER

*Because so many people were coming and going that they
did not even have a chance to eat, he said to them, "Come
with me by yourselves to a quiet place and get some rest."*

—MARK 6:31

When I went to physical therapy to rehabilitate my
arm after surgery, my therapist told me that I
should rest one minute between every set of reps to make
my efforts most beneficial. At first it drove me crazy to sit
there watching the second hand tick on the clock. Resting
between bicep curls only made my routine take longer. But
my therapist explained that rest does two things: it gives our
bodies an opportunity to remove waste produced when we
burn energy and to deliver nutrition to replenish the energy
supply. The harder you work, the more rest time you need
for recovery. That's why athletes take a day off between
lifting weights and runners rest a day or two before a race.
Athletes know they can't achieve peak performance if their
bodies are still trying to recover from previous exertion.

Jesus knew what it was like to have a never-ending stream
of work pressing upon Him. He and His disciples were so
busy tending to the needs around them that they didn't even

have time to eat. Sounds like our lives, doesn't it? We tend to live under the tyranny of the urgent, and sometimes our days can come down to triage (degrees of urgency).

But we can take a page out of Jesus' book here. Despite the unending demands, Jesus and His disciples habitually went away to places where they could be alone and rest. Throughout the Gospel, we see Jesus withdrawing from the crowds, especially after times of demanding ministry such as feeding the five thousand.

Jesus didn't operate under the tyranny of the urgent. He knew it was better to leave pressing things undone to do something more important: rest. Apart from the spiritual benefits of getting alone to spend time with the Father, Jesus was teaching His disciples how to take care of their bodies too. Eventually, if we don't rest between the "reps" in our lives, we will get run-down and reduce our ability to bounce back.

Lord, You had throngs of people to heal and the salvation of the world on Your shoulders—more important work than mine will ever be. Yet You set Your work aside regularly to go to a quiet place and regroup. Help me learn to rest so I can become healthier and can better perform the tasks You set before me.

Seventeen

SELECTIVE REST

*"My food," said Jesus, "is to do the will of him
who set me and to finish his work."*
—JOHN 4:34

Have you ever seen a collection of artwork from a certain era and felt transported—as if you knew what life was like back then? That artwork was carefully chosen by a museum curator to bring that time period to life. These days we often hear advice about "curating" our lives—being choosy about our activities and even belongings, and aligning them with our life's chosen theme. For those of us who follow Jesus, that theme is loving Him and bringing His kingdom to life.

Jesus was the ultimate Curator. He could have done many things as the Son of God, but He stuck to doing the will of His Father. Repeatedly Jesus said He spoke *only* words the Father gave Him and did *only* what His Father asked Him to do. He never tried to pursue His own agenda; instead, He gave up what He wanted in deference to His Father's plan.

When we feel overwhelmed by our schedules, perhaps some curation is in order. Let's learn the difference between limiting ourselves to the work the Father gives us and trying to accomplish the work we have decided to take on ourselves. Feeling as though you have more than can possibly fit into a twenty-four-hour day or barely having enough time to shower or sit down to eat a meal is an indicator that you are overbooked.

If your schedule has pushed you into a corner and squeezed out God, it's time to curate. Sort through your schedule and carefully remove the things that don't belong because God has not put them there. According to Mark Vroegop, lead pastor at College Park Church in Indianapolis, you can get back on track by putting all your *P*s in the right order: *person, partner, parent, parishioner, provider,* and *player.*

Living in a rhythm of work and rest might require sacrifice, but if you think of it as *curation*, it might not seem so difficult. Curation opens an opportunity to trade a harried, hectic schedule for a beautiful collection: time to know the Lord better, purposeful investment in things that will last, deeper relationships instead of a focus on things, and an abiding peace that flows from living according to God's design.

Lord, I feel responsible to make sure everything goes right for my family, my ministry, and myself. Give me the grace to do the work You, my Father, has given me—even if it means curating my collection of activities.

Eighteen

IT IS FINISHED

*After he had provided purification for sins, he sat
down at the right hand of the Majesty in heaven.*
—HEBREWS 1:3

Mission accomplished! Jesus finished the work God gave Him: salvation of the world. And when He had done this, today's verse tells us He "sat down" in heaven at the right hand of God the Father. "Sat down" here comes from a Greek word *kathizo*, which means "rest," the same word used when the Holy Spirit came to rest on believers in Acts 2:3. After completing His work of saving humanity from our sins, Jesus rested. You can almost hear a flourish of trumpets announcing His arrival in heaven as He triumphantly takes His seat on the throne.

Back on Earth, people still needed healing, sinners still needed saving, and even the religious still needed Jesus' teaching. *All* the work of God's kingdom was not done, but Jesus had finished the work God gave *Him*. Jesus proclaimed from the cross, "It is finished" (John 19:30). These words mark the grand finale to Jesus' earthly ministry. In His absence, the Spirit continually works to help us live the Christian life until He returns.

In the same way, even when all the work in our world is not done, we must rest. At the end of the day we must say, "It is finished" and sit down for a while. The challenge is focusing on the work God has given us, not trying to do it all—and not trying to do it all at once.

It takes great faith to rest because we must trust that God will take care of everything left undone. Pastor John Ortberg beautifully describes how to let go of unfinished business with a peaceful heart: "Sleep is a gift from God. . . . The world will get along very well even though I am not awake to try to control things. At the appropriate time, my eyes will open and I will receive the gift of wakefulness once again."[2]

So tonight, close your eyes and rest, praying the trusting words of the psalmist: "The LORD will accomplish what concerns me; Your loving kindness, O LORD, is everlasting; Do not forsake the works of Your hands" (Psalm 138:8 NASB).

Lord, I am forever grateful that Jesus humbled Himself, setting aside all the riches of heaven to come to Earth and die for me. What an example of selfless love and sacrifice. Help me follow His example, let go, and trust completely in You, leaving all my unfinished business in Your hands.

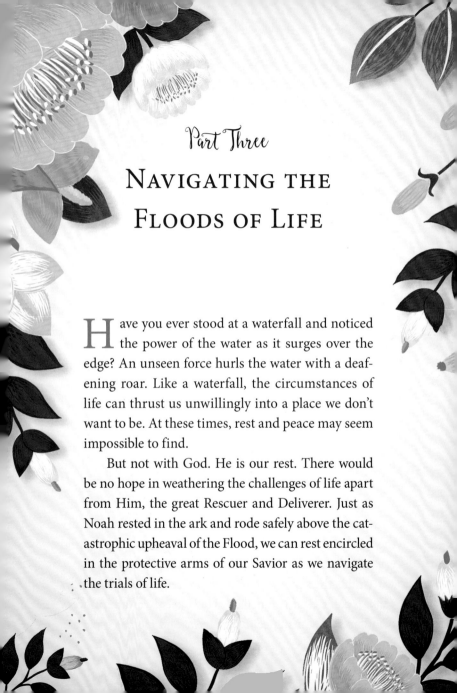

Part Three

NAVIGATING THE FLOODS OF LIFE

Have you ever stood at a waterfall and noticed the power of the water as it surges over the edge? An unseen force hurls the water with a deafening roar. Like a waterfall, the circumstances of life can thrust us unwillingly into a place we don't want to be. At these times, rest and peace may seem impossible to find.

But not with God. He is our rest. There would be no hope in weathering the challenges of life apart from Him, the great Rescuer and Deliverer. Just as Noah rested in the ark and rode safely above the catastrophic upheaval of the Flood, we can rest encircled in the protective arms of our Savior as we navigate the trials of life.

Nineteen

THE LORD SEES

The LORD saw how great the wickedness of the human race had become on the earth, and that every inclination of the thoughts of the human heart was only evil all the time. . . . But Noah found favor in the eyes of the LORD.
—GENESIS 6:5, 8

Circumstances could not have been more dire for Noah. He lived in a world marked by violence, corruption, and every kind of evil imaginable. Utterly alone in a spiritual sense, Noah lived each day as the only human on the face of the earth who walked with God. Imagine the grief he must have experienced watching evil multiply in the society around him. Yet he remained powerless to change his circumstances or others. There was no place for Noah to run and hide.

But the Lord knew what was going on. He *saw* the wickedness. He was keenly aware of every detail and every thought in the hearts of all people. Never turning a blind eye, God had a plan in mind to take care of everything.

God is the same yesterday, today, and forever (Hebrews 13:8). Noah's God is our God. He is keenly aware of every detail and circumstance in our lives, and He has a plan to deal with them. Sometimes our circumstances can seem so overwhelming that all we see is impossibility and forget our sovereign God can handle anything. A friend once told me, "Don't tell God how big your storm is. Tell your storm how big your God is."

Just how big is our God? He is the Creator of the universe. He spoke, and at His command the world came into existence. He is omniscient, which means He knows *everything*—every intimate detail of every part of every heart and every life. He is all-wise, which means He knows exactly what to do about every problem we will ever face. He is powerful enough to send anything we need, including rest and peace, when we feel the waters rise around us.

So if you are stuck in the middle of circumstances that seem too great for you to bear, know that your loving Creator-God bends close to you, listening to your prayers and lifting you up.

> *Lord, bring comfort to my heart. Remind me each moment that You see all that is happening, that You have a perfect plan for dealing with it. Help me to keep my focus on You, "for nothing will be impossible with [You]" (Luke 1:37 ESV).*

Twenty

IN GOD'S HANDS

"Everything on earth will perish. But I will establish my covenant with you, and you will enter the ark—you and your sons and your wife and your sons' wives with you."
—GENESIS 6:17–18

I f you've ever been under the spell of streaming television drama, you know about the technique of the cliff-hanger. Producers use it to keep you bingeing on a show, leaving the next episode to queue up so you can get your questions answered. *There's no way they can get out of that one,* you think. *How could they possibly survive?* Yet the series writers always seem to deliver, no matter how preposterous, a way for the story to carry on and the hero to survive.

Noah was at a low point—a cliff-hanger from which there was no way out. Yet God had already written the story, and as unlikely as it looked, He provided an escape that must have seemed preposterous to Noah and his family: the ark.

God had already laid out the script on this situation. He knew ahead of time His plans to purge the earth, and He prepared to keep Noah safe from the calamity. The world wasn't running wildly and recklessly out of control. God knew exactly what evil humanity was up to, and He knew

Noah needed rescue. God conceived, wrote, and directed a plan for Noah to build an ark, keeping him, his family, and the animals safe from the Flood. As crazy as that plan must have sounded, Noah chose to trust God and to obey Him—to submit to God's plans. And God brought him through.

In the same way, God is intimately familiar with the circumstances that intrude into our lives. We might be on edge, biting our nails over a hopeless-seeming cliff-hanger, but He is not. He knows exactly what to do. We might not know when the situation will resolve or how. We might not understand what will be required of us, why we are being subjected it, or how any good could ever come out of it. What is unknown to us, however, is perfectly known to Him.

God provided plans for an ark to save Noah. He will provide a means of protection and provision for us during our trials too. Will we obey His Word, trusting the Writer of our story even if it seems preposterous? Noah chose to place His future squarely in God's hands, even though He wasn't sure how the details would unfold. Placing our future in God's hands is the only way we will find rest and peace too.

Lord, You are El Roi, *the God who sees me. You are not surprised by my situation because You knew it would happen and already have a plan to help me. Give me faith to rest in You even though I have no idea how it will all work out.*

Twenty-One

PROTECTION FROM
THE STORM

*On that very day Noah and his sons, Shem, Ham and
Japheth, together with his wife and the wives of his three
sons entered the ark. . . . Then the LORD shut him in.*
—GENESIS 7:13, 16

In a storm, a door means security. Whether rain is lashing the side of your house or a stormy sea is rocking your houseboat with pounding waves, a snug seal and secure door will keep you safe from damage or drowning.

The door on Noah's ark must have been particularly heavy-duty. So much so, in fact, that God had to close it Himself. Noah's responsibility was to build and enter the ark, but he was not responsible to keep himself safe; that was God's job. After Noah and his family entered the ark along with all the animals, God shut them in. Securing the door meant safety from the cataclysm outside as the fountains of the deep burst forth and the windows of heaven flung wide open. Noah alone could not have pulled the great entryway closed; God needed to do it for him.

Noah surrendered to God's divine battening down the

hatches when he boarded the ark. We can learn something about surrender from Noah too. With no rudder to steer or any other ability to keep the ark afloat, Noah entrusted his and his family's well-being into His Creator's hands as "He blotted out every living thing that was on the face of the ground, man and animals and creeping things and birds of the heavens. . . . Only Noah was left, and those who were with him in the ark" (Genesis 7:23 ESV).

God preserves us in our storms too. He keeps us safe. Why exhaust ourselves trying to close a door that is too heavy for us to budge when God invites us to rest in Him? He is strong enough to protect us: "The eternal God is your dwelling place, and underneath are the everlasting arms" (Deuteronomy 33:27 ESV). As our Dwelling Place, God is a refuge—a safe place in which to take shelter during the storms of life. If we will allow Him to enfold us in His arms, He will do all the work of holding us close, protecting, and providing.

Lord, I can't save myself from my troubles, but I know that You will never let me go. Even if everything seems to be falling apart, You will carry me through and bring me to restful, calm seas.

47

Twenty-Two

REST IN THE WAITING

[The waters] rose greatly on the earth, and all the high
mountains under the entire heavens were covered. . . . The
waters flooded the earth for a hundred and fifty days.
—Genesis 7:19, 24

While it rained forty days and forty nights, Noah
spent much more time than that on the ark. From
the day rain began falling on the earth until Noah stepped
off the ark onto dry ground, approximately one year had
passed. Scriptures don't tell us what Noah did during that
time, but we know that he waited. He performed the daily
tasks such as feeding the animals and caring for his family.
And he waited.

Waiting can be the hardest part of any trial. Waiting
gives us lots of time to think, wonder, and worry: *When will
it end? What if this or that happens—then what will I do?* In
the waiting room, our worries often grow into giant storm
clouds that threaten to burst forth, initiating the next disaster. But God bids us to wait expectantly and watch for Him
to keep His perfect promises. Waiting doesn't have to breed
paralysis, and fretting doesn't have to spiral or become all-
consuming, keeping us from being present and productive

each day. "Worry does not empty tomorrow of its sorrow. It empties today of its strength," says Corrie ten Boom, a Holocaust survivor who understood the paradox of worry and waiting.[3]

Our waiting time should not be wasted time. Often God allows us to be in His waiting room so we have time to step back from the pressures of life and focus on Him. Our waiting time presents a unique opportunity to draw near to God and rest. All the energy we pour into agonizing over "what ifs" can be replaced by meditating on the character and promises of God:

- "I will never leave you nor forsake you." (Joshua 1:5)
- And we know that in all things God works for the good of those who love him. (Romans 8:28)
- You will keep in perfect peace those whose minds are steadfast, because they trust in you. (Isaiah 26:3)

While our circumstances might not change, we can release our minds and hearts from the entanglement of worry. We can free them to find comfort and rest in God as we keep our focus on Him.

Lord, help me to trust You in my waiting room instead of wringing my hands in worry. Even though I am waiting, I know that You have not put me on hold. Show me how to rest and focus on You.

Twenty-Three

NOT FORGOTTEN

*God remembered Noah and all the wild animals and
the livestock that were with him in the ark, and he
sent a wind over the earth, and the waters receded.*

—GENESIS 8:1

Most children love to play hide-and-seek. I don't know whether it's the thrill of the hunt or the element of surprise, but a good game of hide-and-seek always fills the house with squeals and giggles. Unless, of course, the seeker isn't immediately successful. Tension builds as the search goes on and, if it lasts too long, the game can end in frustration and tears. Even though the child knows his friend is still hiding, he can't bear the thought that he can't find him.

When unwanted circumstances drag on in our lives the way they did for Noah, we can feel as if we can't find God. Our prayers rise up to His throne, but if we don't get a prompt answer, we wonder whether God has forgotten about us. As Noah and his family floated for what must have seemed like endless days in the ark, they could have concluded that God had forgotten about them too.

God is our perfect Father. He doesn't play hide-and-seek, sending us on wild-goose chases until we finally figure out where to find Him. He remains in the same place firmly seated on His throne. Jesus also sits at His right hand praying for us 24/7 along with the Holy Spirit, who especially intercedes for us when we are so exhausted or frustrated that we don't know what to say. When the Scriptures tell us that God "remembered Noah," it doesn't mean Noah had previously slipped God's mind. It means the time had come for God to keep His promises to Noah. After God had accomplished His purposes through the Flood, He sent winds to dry up the waters so Noah could finally return to solid ground. Far from forgetting about Noah, God had been quietly working behind the scenes to take care of Him at every point, even when Noah was unaware.

It might seem our prayers are not finding their way to Him, but we can rest in the fact that He hears and answers every one. In fact, He doesn't wait for us to pray; He's already on the lookout to meet our needs before we ask. So we can rest knowing God is always at work even if He hasn't yet let us in on how He plans to answer our prayers.

Lord, when the skies blacken and rain descends like a curtain, I can't seem to find You in the darkness. As You remembered Noah, remember me. And help me remember You—that You are near, always looking for ways to help me, even before I ask. Let me rest in Your nearness.

51

Twenty-Four

ETERNAL RESULTS

*At the end of the hundred and fifty days the water had
gone down, and on the seventeenth day of the seventh
month the ark came to rest on the mountains of Ararat.*

—GENESIS 8:3–4

After a long, hard winter, nothing is better than seeing crocus buds peeking out from the melting snow. Buttery daffodils, rainbow-hued tulips, and the glorious pink of flowering crab apple trees are soon to follow. New life has been working its magic hidden by the barren, frozen ground. The transformation begins where we can't see it, but it is happening nonetheless.

Long winters do not go on forever, although it sometimes seems as though they'll never end. Perhaps Noah and his family etched marks into the wall of the ark, keeping track of the months they were tossed on the waves. Their confinement must have felt like an eternity, but something unseen was happening while Noah and his family were enduring.

Our trials are a gateway to new beginnings, although they can be difficult to see at the time. As Paul wrote to the Corinthians about his shipwrecks, beatings, imprisonments, and sufferings for Christ, he viewed them this way: "Our light and momentary troubles are achieving for us an eternal glory that far outweighs them all" (2 Corinthians 4:17).

Nothing seems light or momentary about trials—or riding on an ark for months while a cataclysmic Flood wipes out everything. Compared to eternity, however, these trials are like the blink of a cursor on a computer screen. Paul's trials led to new, eternal life as people personally responded to the good news of the gospel. Noah's ordeal yielded eternal results too, as God purged a violent, sin-filled world and promised never to send a worldwide flood again.

God also will accomplish His eternal purposes in our trials, bringing new faith, new trust, new wisdom, new knowledge of His Word, and a fresh experience of His love. When we're in the middle of the fight, we can rest knowing that our hardships will not last forever and will not be in vain. Ask God to open your eyes to see how the trials you are facing can yield eternal, unseen joy. Then you can face them rested and buoyed by His strength.

Thank You, Lord, that my hardships won't last forever. Help me to cling to the hope of Your eternal purpose, and use my trials to make me into what You want me to be. While I face them, fill me with rest and peace in Your plans.

Twenty-Five

A SIGN OF HOPE

"Whenever I bring clouds over the earth and the rainbow
appears in the clouds, I will remember my covenant between
me and you and all living creatures of every kind. Never
again will the waters become a flood to destroy all life."
—GENESIS 9:14–15

The story of Noah and the Flood didn't end when the ark came to rest on Mount Ararat. After Noah and his family disembarked, Noah built an altar and worshipped the Lord. The world he once knew, marred by violence and evil, God had made new. The Flood ended up being a blessing to Noah. God had preserved him and his family when everything else was breaking apart. Noah bowed in grateful adoration to worship his Rescuer and Deliverer. God then made a covenant with Noah, promising never to destroy all life with a flood again and gave him the rainbow as a sign.

God's sign is still comforting to us in the storms of life. The light of His love and the rain of our tears combine to create a beautiful rainbow in the storm. And this kind of rainbow also serves as a sign to others in our lives who are looking for hope.

As people watch God helping you walk through something you could never survive on your own, they will know that He is real. They will know that He is a powerful Miracle Worker. They will know that He is personally involved in the lives of His children. They will see a picture of His grace, love, and mercy. If they are looking for peace and rest in their trials, maybe they will want to know Him too. God displayed His power and glory by saving Noah from the destruction of the Flood, and He will display His power and glory in your life by preserving you and bringing you to a place of peace and rest.

Lord, You make rainbows of beauty out of the worst circumstances. That's because You are a miracle-working God. Please do a miracle in me, and show Your sign of peace and hope to others through it.

Twenty-Six

BETTER PLANS

Because the LORD had closed Hannah's womb,
her rival kept provoking her in order to irritate
her. This went on year after year.
—1 SAMUEL 1:6–7

Hannah was in a horrible predicament. She was one of two wives—the one who couldn't have children while the other wife had many. Her husband loved and cherished her, a small consolation for the relentless taunting she had to endure from wife number two.

Hannah's anguish was multiplied as she bore her unfulfilled longing for a child and her humiliation as the other wife bragged about her fertility. The most devastating part of the situation was that the Lord was responsible: He had closed her womb.

Hannah was not suffering because she sinned or because of some spiritual battle between good and evil. She was suffering because God has chosen not to fulfill her deep longing for a child even though He had the power to do so. No reason is given.

It's painful when God doesn't give us what we want, and He doesn't always explain why. But take comfort in the fact that He always gives what is best. As a loving heavenly Father, He has goals for us that are far different from our own. Of course we want comfort, peace, prosperity, and lives of ease for ourselves and loved ones. Yet God desires so much more for us. He wants to conform us to the image of Christ so we know Him deeply and intimately. He longs for us to experience a fresh outpouring of His love and grace because He knows that will bring us greater fulfillment than having everything we want. He wants us to realize that He truly is all we need. When we have Him, we have everything, which is a profound comfort when our dreams are beyond reach and our self-sufficiency comes to an end.

As we will see, Hannah's desperation ultimately brought her to the Lord, and He ultimately brought her peace and fulfillment. We can find rest in going to the Lord too, with our hands held open to Him so that He can do what's best in our pain. As much as Hannah wanted a baby, her rest would come in accepting His plans, not her own.

Lord, help me remember that when You don't give me what I want, You give me something better—Yourself. As a perfectly wise Father, You know that my deepest longing is for You, because the fulfillment and joy of knowing You far surpasses anything I could have in this world.

Twenty-Seven

POURED OUT

I am a woman who is deeply troubled. I have not been drinking wine or beer; I was pouring out my soul to the LORD. Do not take your servant for a wicked woman; I have been praying here out of my great anguish and grief.

—1 SAMUEL 1:15–16

Years of infertility. Relentless taunting. Social stigma. All these things added up to Hannah's "great anguish and grief." When she went to the temple to pray that day, she was truly at the end of her rope. After she exhausted all her coping mechanisms, she turned to the Lord and poured out her heart to Him. What came out was not pretty. The priest at the temple where she prayed even thought she was drunk! But Hannah held nothing back. Years of pent-up tears and pain burst forth like water rupturing a dam.

We can learn a lesson from Hannah when we are overwhelmed too. To find emotional rest, pour out the contents of your heart before God; don't bottle them up. Friends and a support system can be wonderful to rely on in challenging times, but no one can give you true peace from inner turmoil the way God, the Maker of your heart, can. He already knows what you are feeling, even the "ugly" emotions of bitterness, jealousy, anger, grief, hopelessness, and unbelief. We must be honest with God and with ourselves. Remaining trapped in the prison of our overwhelming feelings will keep us separated from the Source of true peace. So open up in prayer, and let everything flood out before the One who loves you. Even writing thoughts to God in a journal can release them from the tangled swirl in your mind and give them a black-and-white reality so they can be tamed.

Scripture promises peace will follow our heartfelt prayers: "Do not be anxious about anything, but in every situation, by prayer and petition, with thanksgiving, present your requests to God. And the peace of God, which transcends all understanding, will guard your hearts and your minds in Christ Jesus" (Philippians 4:6–7). Present those requests, even if they spill out in a messy, haphazard way. God is waiting to lead you from a place of grief to peace—a supernatural peace. Even if our circumstances don't change immediately, we can know with 100 percent confidence that God is with us. And He stays with us, our loving Father, while we open up to Him, no matter what comes out.

> *God, You don't want me to stay in turmoil when You can give me perfect peace. Give me the courage to let my feelings out so You have room to come in.*

Twenty-Eight

A NEW DREAM

*LORD Almighty, if You will only look upon your
servant's misery and remember me, and not forget
your servant but give her a son, then I will give
him to the LORD for all the days of his life.*

—1 SAMUEL 1:11

L et go, and let God. Perhaps you've received this classic
advice from a family member, heard it in church, or
even seen it cross-stitched on a pillow. But it's not just a plat-
itude. When we surrender control, we also give our burdens
to God.

As Hannah poured out her heart to God at the temple,
she began to let go. All the years she had struggled with
infertility had come to a head and had slowly transformed
her heart. This time she no longer prayed for her own desire
for a child, but for God's purposes to be fulfilled. She asked
God for a son whom she could dedicate to His service as a
priest. Perhaps Hannah had heard reports about the reck-
less behavior of the current priests and knew a godly man
was needed to serve before Him.

In her prayer, Hannah traded her misery for something
much bigger, an opportunity to fulfill God's broader plan.

Sometimes we forget God has a broader plan when we are drowning in our own sorrow. We can get tunnel vision and lose sight of the many other ways God can bring about blessing in our lives. Griefs in this world can be overwhelming, but they are not beyond the power of God to transform into serving His greater purposes and even bringing us joy. Therein lies our hope. When Hannah was able to let go of the painful disappointment of her situation, God lifted it from her shoulders and gave her a new vision.

Like Hannah, we can relinquish the turmoil and unrest that come from trying to bring about what we want. Instead, we can ask God to change us so we will be content and desire what He wants. Then perhaps our trials will seem less like battering storms and more like instruments God uses to change our hearts and bring us to ultimate rest in Him. "'I know the plans I have for you,' declares the LORD, 'plans to prosper you and not to harm you, plans to give you hope and a future'" (Jeremiah 29:11).

Father, I don't want You to give me what I want if it means I will miss something far greater. Help me surrender my hardships to You and trust that You will bring about the best outcome as only You, my almighty God, can.

61

Twenty-Nine

CHANGED FROM WITHIN

Eli answered, "Go in peace, and may the God of Israel grant you what you have asked of him." She said, "May your servant find favor in your eyes." Then she went her way and ate something, and her face was no longer downcast.

—1 SAMUEL 1:17–18

In 1875, another Hannah—activist Hannah Whitall Smith—wrote about changes of the heart. She said, "It is wonderful what miracles God works in wills that are utterly surrendered to Him. He turns hard things into easy, and bitter things into sweet. It is not that He puts easy things in place of the hard, but He actually changes the hard thing into an easy one."[4] In the Bible, Hannah experienced this change. She walked away from her cathartic prayer session as a new person. The priest Eli could see it on her face: she was "no longer downcast."

Hannah, however, didn't have a child in her arms. She was still living with another wife who provoked her for being childless. While her circumstances hadn't changed, Hannah had. She had committed the situation into God's hands and could move forward in peace. Whether God answers our prayers by giving us the desires of our hearts, or we move forward in faith not knowing the outcome, we can rest once we have surrendered the situation to God.

Not knowing what will happen but trusting in God, Noah built the ark, climbed aboard with his family, and watched as God closed him in. Both Noah and Hannah took refuge in the "ark" of His protection and presence, where they could rest as they rode out the storms of life.

Hannah's years of waiting eventually resulted in a son. When he was old enough, Hannah kept her vow and took him to the temple where he spent the rest of his life serving the Lord. God also blessed her with more children. What initially appeared to be a disaster God turned to blessing—not only for Hannah but also for the nation of Israel. Just as He displayed His glory through saving Noah from the Flood and raising up a godly leader from Hannah's infertility, He can bring good and glory out of any circumstance in our lives. He can turn bitter into sweet and turmoil into unshakeable peace. But first, He changes our hearts.

Lord, I cannot see the ultimate end of my trials, but You can. Help me to trust Your good purposes. When I can't change my circumstances, change me.

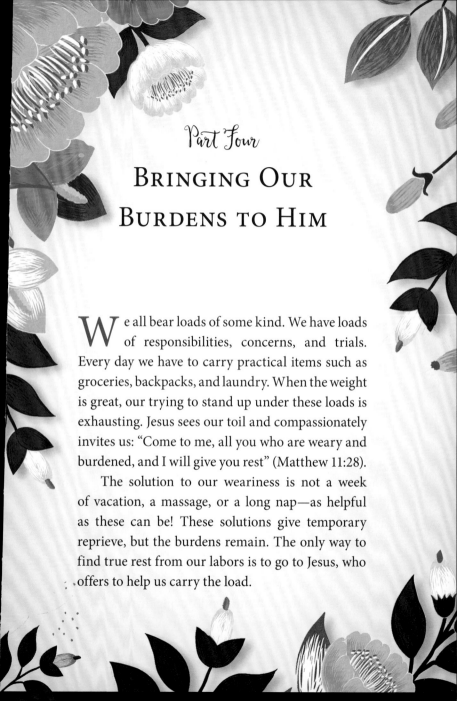

Part Four

BRINGING OUR BURDENS TO HIM

We all bear loads of some kind. We have loads of responsibilities, concerns, and trials. Every day we have to carry practical items such as groceries, backpacks, and laundry. When the weight is great, our trying to stand up under these loads is exhausting. Jesus sees our toil and compassionately invites us: "Come to me, all you who are weary and burdened, and I will give you rest" (Matthew 11:28).

The solution to our weariness is not a week of vacation, a massage, or a long nap—as helpful as these can be! These solutions give temporary reprieve, but the burdens remain. The only way to find true rest from our labors is to go to Jesus, who offers to help us carry the load.

Thirty

THE INVITATION

"Come to me, all who you who are weary and
burdened, and I will give you rest."
—MATTHEW 11:28

P erhaps you know the relief of finally setting down an overweight suitcase, a huge sack of groceries, or even a chubby toddler after hours of carrying. That's the wonderful thing about physical burdens: you can put them down, catch your breath, and pick them up again if needed. What about internal burdens—the ones we can't put down and walk away from?

Having had three different kinds of cancer (the first diagnosis came in college), I have been weary and burdened most of my adult life. I've felt like a ship navigating to my final destination, but no matter where I go, unwanted cargo continually seems to be heaped on. Many times I thought I would sink, but Jesus has always rescued me and invited me to rest. He can do the same for you.

In today's verse, Jesus has handwritten a personal invitation to you and to me. With gentle lovingkindness, He calls us to come to Him and receive His gift of rest. He is strong enough to hold any burden no matter how large, so we can sink into His loving arms and catch our breath.

The weight of the world might be on your shoulders, or your world might be falling apart. You might be exhausted to the bone, too tired to pick yourself up or to take a step forward. Your energy might be sapped as one thing has piled onto another. Jesus can hold you up, and He can hold you together. Nothing is too difficult for Him. Jesus is waiting, just waiting, for you to come to Him. Whether you reach out in prayer, in thanksgiving, in silent waiting, in reading through His Word, or in an instantaneous cry from the driver's seat as you wait for a green light, He invites you to turn to Him. Don't struggle on your own one minute longer. He has an endless supply of Kleenex to dry your tears and inexhaustible strength to infuse your weary bones. There's nothing in the world like Jesus' rest and renewal to make you able to move forward again.

Lord, thank You that I am never a burden to You. You invite me to come to You over and over again, as often as I need to come. When I can't find rest anywhere else, I know I will always find it in You.

Thirty-One

TREADING WATER

*"Lord, if it's you," Peter replied, "tell me to come to
you on the water." "Come," he said. Then Peter got
down out of the boat, walked on the water and came
toward Jesus. But when he saw the wind, he was afraid
and, beginning to sink, cried out, "Lord, save me!"*
—MATTHEW 14:28–30

Few things are more relaxing than paddling a kayak on open water, chasing dragonflies, and watching the turtles play—unless it's a *very blustery* day. I learned this the hard way. I figured strong winds and waves might even be fun the day I hopped into the kayak. After struggling to get halfway across the lake, muscles burning under the strain of keeping upright against the strong wind and waves, I began rehearsing scenarios about what I could do if I ran out of strength to paddle back to shore. I was never more thankful to have a life vest on board.

If you find the strain of paddling against the current of life is exhausting, you can count on the ultimate Life Preserver to save you: Jesus. As He did for Peter, He will come to you when you cry out, "Lord, save me!"

After feeding the five thousand, Jesus told His disciples

to get in a boat and head to the other side of the lake. Then He left them and went up on a mountainside by Himself to pray. When gale-force winds unexpectedly struck the boat that night, Jesus, knowing everything, was aware of the disciples' fear. He saw them struggling to keep the boat from capsizing, so He went to them, walking on the water.

Imagine their surprise! To be certain it wasn't a ghost, Peter asked Jesus to allow him to walk toward Him on the water. The moment he looked away from Jesus to the wind and the waves, Peter began to sink, fearing for His life. But He had his Life Preserver at his side, and He was all Peter needed to save him.

Jesus is moved by our grief and burdens. He knows when we come to the point of exhaustion, straining to keep upright when life's gale-force winds push against us. As He saw the disciples struggling when He was on the mountainside praying, the all-knowing, ever-present Son of God sees us even when we are unaware of His presence. He longs to hear our cry for help. Our prayer simply can be, "Lord, save me," and He will come running with a life preserver to hold us up.

Lord, when I feel as if I'm drowning, help me look up and see You, unbothered by the waves, steadily coming toward me with sure footing to reach out and take hold of me. You have the strength to carry me to rest and safety.

Thirty-Two

THE EASY YOKE

"Take my yoke upon you. . . . For my yoke
is easy and my burden is light."
—MATTHEW 11:29–30

I n Nepal, most of the field laborers spend their days bent over, doing backbreaking work by hand. You can imagine how these rural farmers prize even the most rudimentary plow and a pair of oxen. When yoked together by a simple harness of rough-hewn wood, two oxen can plow acres of hardened, rock-strewn soil in a single afternoon.

Jesus' solution when we need to bear up under impossibly heavy burdens is taking what He calls His yoke so we don't have to pull the full weight on our own. When we're yoked with Him, Jesus can summon all the power of heaven and Earth to help us conquer what we could never do alone. When Jesus eases the load, He makes the heavy wooden yoke feel light.

But the benefit of being yoked to Jesus comes with a price tag. A free-roaming ox must forego wandering in its pasture to be yoked for plowing. In the same way, we must be willing to give up our freedom to take Jesus' yoke. Every Nepali farmer knows that unless the oxen work together, the plow will tip over. To experience welcome relief from our burdens, we need to keep lockstep with Jesus. This is a beautiful place to be—in His yoke, near His heart, and aware of every small adjustment He makes to lighten the load as much as possible. The relief we feel will be worth the trade, our surrender for the nearness and power of God's Son.

Our willingness to set aside our agenda for His plans, His timing, His pace, and His direction will guide us into the yoke a little more easily. When we feel the yoke—obedience to Jesus—rubbing us the wrong way, we might need to correct our path and realign with His purposes and commands. This will seem easier if we focus on the seeds God can plant in the fresh furrows of broken-up ground to produce new fruit in our lives. Yes, the yoke is a place of surrender, but it's also the way Jesus lifts our burdens and allows us to rest.

Lord, I know the field ahead is impossible for me to plow alone, but not if I am yoked to You, the all-powerful God of the universe. All the uncertainties ahead won't matter if I follow Your lead and keep in step with You.

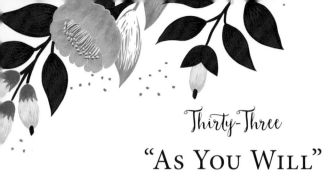

Thirty-Three

"As You Will"

*Going a little farther, he fell with his face to the ground
and prayed, "My Father, if it is possible, may this cup
be taken from me. Yet not as I will, but as you will."*
—MATTHEW 26:39

Not only a heavy wooden beam. Not only the pain of His wounds. Jesus carried a burden greater than any we will ever be asked to carry. The Father asked Jesus, His sinless, holy Son, to be crucified to pay for the sins of the world. Jesus' mission meant humiliation, rejection, excruciating physical suffering, emotional anguish, and the injustice of receiving punishment He didn't deserve. Jesus didn't want to do it, but He was willing to do His Father's will anyway.

Yet, as today's verse shows, Jesus prayed that God would spare Him from going to the cross. His soul was "overwhelmed with sorrow to the point of death" (Matthew 26:38). As Jesus prayed, His sweat was "like drops of blood falling to the ground" (Luke 22:44). In his humanity, Jesus felt the weight of suffering as it coincided with obedience just as we do.

Jesus is our example in all things, including His grief. He shows us it is okay to ask God to take us from our trials, to spare us from the suffering ahead. Jesus did. It's okay to cry out to God, to beg Him again and again to rescue us. Jesus did.

If we are going to find rest, however, let's not neglect the second part of Jesus' prayer: "Yet not as I will, but as you will." This is a prayer of surrender. We are telling God that we don't want to be where He has placed us, but we are willing to move forward no matter the cost because He is God and will sovereignly take care of us.

Until we are willing to surrender, we will not rest. A part of us will always try to find a way out or be filled with dread over our fates. Coming to the point of surrender is an arduous journey, but the most beautiful place to arrive. Surrender is an unshakable confidence that whatever happens—whether I'm rescued or must shoulder my burdens and walk on—God will sustain me. When I believe that, I will be able to rest.

Jesus, when my burdens seem too heavy to carry, I look to You. The Father led You through the unthinkable agony of the cross. If He had the power to preserve You and raise You from the dead, then He has the power to sustain me too. Because You suffered, You know how to lead me through.

Thirty-Four

HELP ALONG THE WAY

Jesus told his disciples, "If anyone would come after me, let him deny himself and take up his cross and follow me."
—MATTHEW 16:24 ESV

When we're trudging through deep snow, it's always easier to follow footsteps left by someone who walked before us instead of cutting a new trail through knee-high drifts. We benefit from the one who has traveled the path before because he has done the hard work of packing down the snow.

Jesus blazed a trail with His long, arduous journey to the cross, doing the hard work so we could follow behind more easily. He bore up under the burden of fulfilling God's plan in a sin-filled world but rose victorious in the end. We too can be assured of joy and victory at the end of our journey if we are willing to follow in His steps. His path ultimately leads to a place of rest.

Although Jesus' way meant self-denial, setting aside His will for His Father's, He didn't carry His cross alone. On the way to Golgotha where Jesus was crucified, God sent someone unexpected to bear His load. Because Jesus was too weak to carry the crossbeam, a stranger traveling to Jerusalem, Simon of Cyrene, was enlisted to help.

Sometimes our help will come from the most unlikely places when we grow too weak to walk the path God has chosen. He might send relief through a friend who offers to cook a meal, a neighbor who unexpectedly shovels your driveway, or an odd job that "just happens" to come up to provide money needed to pay a bill. Relief also can come directly from God Himself when we read a Bible verse or hear a sermon or a song that seems to gives us precisely the encouragement we need. God delights to surprise us in the ways He makes our path more bearable so we know the help comes from Him.

When you are struggling to follow in His footsteps, resist the urge to veer off course and escape. The way will be so much harder if you rebel and try to make your own trail. Stay on the path of Jesus no matter how difficult the journey. His way leads to heavenly rest and contains hidden sources of help when your own resources have come to an end.

Father, thank You for Jesus, who leads me to You and Your heavenly rest. When the road is marked with suffering, help me to stay the course and trust that You will send help, even if I can't imagine where it will come from. To enter Your rest will be worth it in the end.

Thirty-Five

NOT ALONE

"Take my yoke upon you and learn from me,
for I am gentle and humble in heart."
—MATTHEW 11:29

*I feel so alone. . . . The walls seem to be closing in on me. . . .
No one else understands what I am going through. . . .*
Although we might not realize it, these feelings of isolation
are a normal part of the human experience when bearing
the burden of suffering. Satan's most-used tool is deceiv-
ing us into thinking we are the only ones in the world who
have ever endured such a plight. The Enemy hopes our feelings of isolation will lead to despair, because he knows we
won't call upon Jesus if we think our situation is hopeless.
Even if no one in the world understands, Jesus does. He's
been there.

Suffering was an integral part of Jesus' life. When He
says, "Learn from me," He is in essence saying, "Learn from
someone who has been there." Jesus knows firsthand about
suffering in this fallen world. He made the ultimate sacrifice, giving up His life. And as the sinless Son of God, Jesus
handled His pain in a perfect way. Therefore, He is qualified

as *the* foremost Expert to teach us how to handle anguish and bear up under the heavy weight of burdens.

The book of Hebrews tells us that although He was God's Son, "he learned obedience from the things he suffered" (Hebrews 5:8 NLT). We learn obedience, among many other things, by watching the way He endured. Jesus also teaches us to cling to the Father and trust in His plan because God has the power to bring ultimate blessing from our trials even when we can't see how.

Thankfully, Jesus does not teach us as a stern taskmaster. After telling us to learn from Him, Jesus immediately reminds us that He is "gentle and humble in heart." Even if you have created heartache for yourself though poor choices, Jesus does not condemn you. On the contrary! Jesus will answer when you call, greet you with His comforting heart, forgive you, and teach you how to walk down a new path so you can find rest for your soul.

Jesus stands alongside us in His humanity as a fellow sufferer. Remembering that Jesus struggled can be one of our greatest comforts. Because Jesus shares in our suffering, we are never alone.

Jesus, I've often felt I had no one to talk to who would understand. But You have always been there, even when I couldn't see or feel You. Thank You that I am never alone. Thank You for always understanding.

Thirty-Six

REST FROM ANXIETY

"You will find rest for your souls."
—MATTHEW 11:29

What a glorious promise! Soul rest seems to be the hardest to find. Physically we might be able to pull ourselves away from the pressures of the world and retreat to a quiet place where we can still our bodies and unplug from the noise. Although our bodies can be at rest, our minds often keep running. Finding physical rest is one thing, but reining in the anxious thoughts constantly swirling through our minds is another matter.

Jesus promises rest for both our bodies and our souls. In the text surrounding today's verse, He tells us to come to Him when we're weary and burdened. Jesus wants to take the weight off our shoulders and hold it for us, giving us an opportunity to rest and regroup. But Jesus doesn't stop there. He promises an even deeper soul rest if we also are willing to take His yoke and learn from Him. Rest for our souls requires surrender—and giving up control and emptying ourselves is a process. Sometimes we need to cry out to God again and again: "Help me overcome my unbelief!" (Mark 9:24). When we reach the point of trust and surrender, our souls can stop fretting. A new mantra replaces the worries and fears whirling through our hearts: *I don't know what is going to happen, but Jesus has this.*

A mind uncluttered by worry is set free to rest. Quiet calm in our souls gives us a chance to simply be in the presence of God and experience renewal, no words needed. After all, Jesus Himself is our true Source of rest. Even if we must continue to carry our burdens, He promises to walk alongside us and lift the load, lightening it so we can rest. In the meantime, we can look forward to heaven where God promises all our burdens and tears will be wiped away.

Lord, fear and worry are inseparable companions, and trying to meet their constant demands exhausts me. Thank You that I do not have to try to drive them away alone. You arm me with the weapons I need for victory: trust and surrender. Fill my heart with trust in You, so there is no room for anything else.

Thirty-Seven

PEACE IN THE SUFFERING

*"Peace I leave with you; my peace I give you. I do
not give to you as the world gives. Do not let your
hearts be troubled and do not be afraid."*

—JOHN 14:27

I have a sarcoma. It was my third bout with cancer, and
I felt as if the earth were crumbling beneath my feet.
After getting over the shock of facing yet another kind of
cancer (I'd previously had Hodgkin's lymphoma and breast
cancer), I began a new battle to surrender to God. I wanted
rest and peace in my heart, but I could not find it. Honestly, I
wanted to give up. I knew I didn't have the energy or strength
for another cancer battle.

I had plenty of time to think during the two-hundred-
mile round-trip drives from my house to the hospital
where I was treated. As I passed miles and miles of corn-
fields, God brought peace to my troubled heart.

Why does a farmer go through the backbreaking work
of plowing new ground to set furrows in his fields? So he can
plant seeds and eventually reap a harvest. In allowing the
sarcoma, God was inviting me to yoke myself to Him and
plow new ground so I could bear fruit. I had a choice to make:

I could give up because the burden was too great for me, or I could go to Him, take His yoke, put my shoulder to the plow, and trust that something new and worthwhile would result. While riding in the car, I determined to leave the green field of my current happy life, to surrender my heart, and to plow beside Him in the sarcoma field—a place I didn't want to go . . . a place I had to recommit repeatedly to stay.

After making that commitment, my fears began to fade, and God's peace washed over me. God opened my eyes to see that He does not ask us to plow in a hard field to break us but to bless us. Eventually, we will become more fruitful as we learn how to be completely dependent on Him, not on ourselves. He alone gives us a peace that the world knows nothing about as we cling to Him.

Trade your worries for the calm of His presence. Reach for His peace as a lifeline when everything is falling apart. Even if you don't understand why you are suffering, you know Him—and you can rest in the fact that He knows what He is doing.

Lord, I am Your child, and You are my Father. I come to You with a simple childlike faith, admitting that I will never be able to fully comprehend Your ways. Calm me with your peace. Hold me close as I climb up onto Your lap, nestle my head upon Your heart, and rest.

Thirty-Eight

ETERNAL PERSPECTIVE

*"The eternal God is your refuge, and
underneath are the everlasting arms."*
—DEUTERONOMY 33:27

I magine a newborn nestled safely within his mother's arms. As she looks down at her infant contentedly asleep, she dreams about his future and wonders what adventures lie ahead. She pulls him even closer to savor the moment, calling to mind the words her own mother said: *Treasure this time. He will grow up fast.*

We all know life goes quickly, sometimes so quickly we can barely keep up. But not our trials. They seem agonizingly slow. When we have burdens to carry, it can seem as if we're on a road that will never end. At times like these, we can renew our strength by seeing life from God's perspective. James says it well: "You are a mist that appears for a little while and then vanishes" (James 4:14). How easily we forget that Earth is not our final destination. For those who have trusted in Christ alone to forgive their sins, heaven will be their true home for eternity.

While we live bound by space and time, God does not. He always has been and always will be. Taking refuge in Him is the safest place to be in trials. While a mother can hold her child in her arms while he is an infant, before he grows too heavy to carry, God holds us close to keep us safe our entire lives. Undergirding our lives from beginning to end, as today's verse teaches us, are His everlasting arms. No tempest, no force of nature, no circumstance can pull us from His embrace. We are held securely in His protective arms eternally.

That's why rest is so important when we are undergoing trials. Rest allows us to take a time-out from living in survival mode and focus on our heavenly Father. What a welcome relief, to set down our burdens and sink into His everlasting arms. When we are this close to Him, we can hear His voice reminding us that life is a vapor.

Looking heavenward toward our Father is often the difference between losing heart and finding the courage and strength to carry on. As John MacArthur said, "Endurance is based on a person's ability to look beyond the physical to the spiritual, beyond the present to the future, and beyond the visible to the invisible."[5] Today let's remember that God's everlasting arms are around us and that He will carry us safely home.

Lord, thank You for loving me enough to make me ready
for heaven, even if it means putting me through the fire.
Help me to rest and remember that my final destination
will be worth whatever it takes to get there. Thank You
that Your everlasting arms will hold me all the way.

Thirty-Nine

WAITING FOR RENEWAL

Those who wait on the LORD shall renew their strength.
—ISAIAH 40:31 NKJV

We wait all the time—in traffic, in line, for a call, for a response to an e-mail or text, for a package to arrive, for vacation. This ordinary kind of waiting is just part of life. When you believe in God, however, you can also wait with purpose; you can wait *on the Lord.* Waiting on the Lord means we are not arbitrarily and needlessly wasting time. Rather we are at a standstill with an eager and patient expectation that God will act on our behalf. Waiting in this way is a form of rest.

When we wait on the Lord in prayer to fulfill His promises, the time is not pointless. God uses that time to renew our strength. Instead of feeling caught in haphazard circumstances, we hope in the sovereign God who is always working to bring about His best for us. Perhaps waiting is His built-in mechanism to keep our world from running so fast that it spins out of control. Life won't always be easy, but we can rest in the assurance God will be there to give us new strength when we reach the end of our own.

Take this promise to heart: "The LORD is the everlasting God, the Creator of the ends of the earth. He will not grow tired or weary, and his understanding no one can fathom. He gives strength to the weary and increases the power of the weak" (Isaiah 40:28–29). What an incredible assurance. We never have to worry about falling apart because He is always there to give us strength. All we have to do is sit quietly, wait, rest, and be renewed, placing our hope in Him to make us strong.

Lord, whether I like it or not, waiting puts me on pause. How desperately I need to do that so I don't spin out of control. Please make sure my waiting time is not wasted time. Use it as an opportunity to rest and renew me and refocus my heart on You.

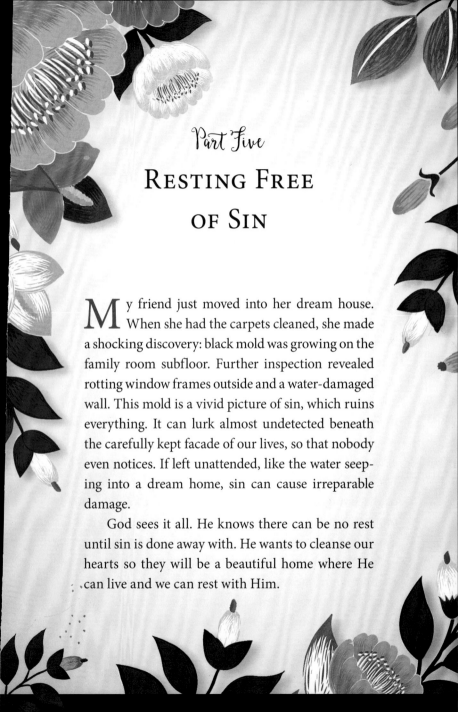

Part Five

RESTING FREE
OF SIN

My friend just moved into her dream house. When she had the carpets cleaned, she made a shocking discovery: black mold was growing on the family room subfloor. Further inspection revealed rotting window frames outside and a water-damaged wall. This mold is a vivid picture of sin, which ruins everything. It can lurk almost undetected beneath the carefully kept facade of our lives, so that nobody even notices. If left unattended, like the water seeping into a dream home, sin can cause irreparable damage.

God sees it all. He knows there can be no rest until sin is done away with. He wants to cleanse our hearts so they will be a beautiful home where He can live and we can rest with Him.

The Quest for Rest

*"Be strong and courageous, because you
will lead these people to inherit the land I
swore to their ancestors to give them."*
—Joshua 1:6

E very epic quest has peril, an evil villain, an insurmountable problem, a hero, and a spectacular ending when all is made right. Joshua and the Israelites' quest to enter God's rest is no exception. Before they could dwell with God in the land where He promised them rest, they had to drive out the enemies living there. They faced the peril of walled cities, expertly trained soldiers, superior weaponry, and an enemy who knew they were coming. But none of that mattered because God was on their side. He exhorted Joshua as the Israelites' leader to be strong and courageous—not terrified or discouraged in the face of what seemed like unbeatable odds. God promised to be with them to help them overcome every peril on their quest as long as they obeyed His words.

In the same way, we face a battle with sin, our great enemy, in our quest to enter God's rest. We are in danger of missing the extraordinary blessing of God's rest because sin separates us from God. Like the Israelites, we do not have to face our battle alone, as God sent the ultimate Hero, Jesus Christ, who is the *only One* who can clear the enemy of sin from the land of our hearts. Just as God saved Joshua and the Israelites from their adversaries, Jesus' death and resurrection can save all people completely from the wrath due them for their sins. We win the battle by obeying God's command to repent (turning away from our sins), receiving Christ's gift of forgiveness, and walking in the power He gives us to lead new lives. Then we can enter His rest.

Our Hero makes all things right in the end. Jesus' death and resurrection wash away the sin in our hearts, restore our relationship with God, and regenerate us to make us new from the inside out. He knows we could never win this battle alone, so He does the fighting for us. What a relief! And He continues to fight for us our whole lives in our quest to drive out the enemies of sin that creep in over time and try to get in the way of our relationship with God. We can rest knowing we have a Hero in Jesus who saves us.

Father, help me to be strong and courageous—knowing You will give me victory to wage all-out war against anything that keeps me from You. I invite You to cleanse my heart and gratefully receive Your gift of forgiveness so I can be at rest.

Forty-One

WITH US ALWAYS

*The LORD replied, "My Presence will go
with you, and I will give you rest."*
—EXODUS 33:14

Nothing is more frustrating than running into a road-block. Detours eat up precious time, not to mention the frustration of being rerouted when you could take the direct route to your destination. Inevitably you will end up behind a semitruck or an uncertain driver who slows your way. Sin is like a roadblock in our lives; it separates us from God's best and easier way.

God has desired to be with us since the beginning—since Adam and Eve. But to be with us, He had to deal with sin because a holy God can't stay in the presence of evil. We can trace His moves against sin through the Bible, from Adam and Eve's exit from the garden, to the great Flood, to the dramatic rescue of the Israelites from Egypt. As He was poised to take them into Canaan, the Promised Land of rest, the roadblock of sin threatened to obstruct their way. No sooner had God finished giving Moses the Ten Commandments than the Israelites violated the first one by making a golden calf to worship in place of God. Calling them a stubborn, "stiff-necked" people, God said He would no longer go with them to the land (Exodus 32:9). Heartbroken, Moses intervened by praying for the people. He asked God to honor his personal obedience to follow Him as the leader of the people and go with them anyway. That brings us to today's verse, when God promised for His presence to go with them, to take them to the Promised Land and give them rest.

We hate to admit it, but we can be like the Israelites. We want to go our own way and do our own thing instead of following God's commands. And that's sin. Things might seem to work for a while, but the roadblock of our sin detours us into heartache and separates us from God and His rest. When you realize you are on the wrong route—we all find ourselves there at some point—don't despair. As Moses did for the Israelites, you have someone who intercedes for you: Jesus. He is always in God's presence praying for us to avoid the roadblock of sin and to return to the route of obedience when we have gotten off course. He wants nothing more than for His presence to be with you and for you to experience His rest. Ask Him to remove your roadblocks today.

Lord, how easy it is for me to get off track and go my own way. I don't want to take a harder route when I could know Your rest. Show me how to live in obedience to You so I don't miss a single moment of Your presence.

91

Forty-Two

ALL THINGS NEW

Therefore, if anyone is in Christ, he is a new creation.
The old has passed away; behold, the new has come.
—2 CORINTHIANS 5:17 ESV

My daughter and I love to watch chick flicks, and *The Guardian* is one of our favorites. In the movie, Kevin Costner turns a class of new recruits into skilled rescuers for the United States Coast Guard. Of course one of the young men falls in love with a girl along the way. We were immediately hooked by the opening scene where Costner, in dramatic fashion, grabs a couple from the jaws of death on the stormy seas. At first it appears that one of the victims does not survive, but Costner breathes life into her water-logged lungs.

New life. A chance to begin again. A savior to make all things new. We love hope-laced stories. Something inside us longs to be made new too. Jesus' work to rescue us from the jaws of sin and death makes a new beginning possible for me and you.

The Bible says that in a spiritual sense we were dead until "God, who is rich in mercy, made us alive with Christ even when we were dead in transgressions" (Ephesians

2:4–5). This is good news! That's why we call it *the gospel*, which means "good news." Jesus, because He loves us, takes our sin and shame and trades them for a brand-new spiritual life.

This means we are never hopelessly stuck in bad habits or negative patterns of behavior. We no longer have to cringe with shame over decisions we've made in the past. God is a God of second chances. With Him we can begin again. While we can't erase the past or sin's consequences, we have hope of moving forward into a new future if we allow Jesus to take away our sins and breathe His life into us.

Be encouraged every morning you look out your window and watch the sunrise. This is God's gift of a new day. When the sun goes down and you are heading off to bed, especially if it was a particularly hard day, be encouraged that tomorrow is a new day. "Because of the LORD's great love we are not consumed, for his compassions never fail. They are new every morning; great is your faithfulness" (Lamentations 3:22–23).

> *Lord, You can make all things new, even my stubborn heart. When I fail, let me rest in Your promise to give me a new day and all the help I need to begin again.*

93

Forty-Three

ERASING SIN

For as high as the heavens are above the earth, so great is his love for those who fear him; as far as the east is from the west, so far has he removed our transgressions from us.

—PSALM 103:11–12

Before laptops and flat screens made it into the classroom, teachers taught the old-fashioned way—they used chalkboards and chalk. Students back then participated the old-fashioned way too. At the end of the day, they would wiggle in their seats, raising their hands high for the privilege of being called on to erase the board. Sometimes that was the best part of the day: seeing all the schoolwork vanish just before the bell rang and everyone could head home.

Our sins are not permanent. They can be erased too. Today's verse tells us that when God forgives us He removes our sins "as far as the east is from the west." Exactly how far is that? If we started today and headed west in hopes of arriving east, we would still be traveling an eternity from now. God takes our sins so far away that we will never see them again.

If He forgets them, why do we keep bringing them up? Carrying the heavy weight of our sins robs us of rest. It can be exhausting to beat ourselves up repeatedly for our failures or to carry around loads of regret. Even worse is carrying around the weight of bitterness and resentment against someone who has sinned against us. God tells us, "Forgive as the Lord forgave you" (Colossians 3:13). God has forgiven us completely, so that is what He requires of us. Forgiveness can be easier to offer if you remember that it does not mean you are saying what the other person did was okay. When you forgive another, you are saying that you are willing to give up getting even with her. You are agreeing with God that it's His job to handle payment for that person's sins, not yours.

If you are carrying the weight of your own sin or someone's sin against you, set it down today and rest. Ask Jesus to forgive you and to take away those sins, far, far away, where they will never resurface again. Ask Him to erase them from the replay reel in your mind and replace them with restful thoughts of His mercy and grace.

Lord, You erase every smudge of my sin with Your forgiveness, without leaving even a trace. Thank You that You don't hold my sins against me. It's a wonderful feeling to rest, knowing I am forgiven.

Forty-Four

CLEANSING SABBATH

*"In repentance and rest is your salvation, in
quietness and trust is your strength."*
—ISAIAH 30:15

F asting from the Internet or social media is becoming
more and more popular these days. People are realizing
that they need a mental break from "an anxious mind, eyes
weary with longing, and a despairing heart" (Deuteronomy
28:65). If this doesn't sound like life in our world today, I
don't know what does. Picture-perfect posts give us feelings
of envy and inadequacy. It all feels so empty. No wonder
we're turning away from the screens around us!

Consider taking a Sabbath rest from the noise of the
world. On the Sabbath we sit still in the quiet and come
before God. We turn our hearts to Him and His purity, asking Him to reveal and forgive the sin in our lives. This not
only restores us, it keeps the chaos and emptiness of the world
from overtaking us.

When we look at all the turmoil in the world as it streams
through our news feeds, we're seeing the result of sin left to
spiral out of control, unaddressed before God. Today's verse
describes how we can refresh and renew our hope: repent.

Sometimes repentance brings to mind images of a preacher pounding the pulpit and God sending down fire and brimstone. Repentance is actually a quiet activity of the heart. When we repent, we decide to stop heading in the direction of the world and make a U-turn to go in the direction of God. Repentance means turning from the behavior that God as a loving Father will discipline, if left unchecked, to get us back on track.

Even though Christ ultimately saves us from our sin, we are prone to wander. Let's admit it, some element of sin holds an immediate attraction or pleasure, or we wouldn't sin. But underneath lurks utter ruin, which God wants to spare us from. Approaching your Sabbath rest with repentance is one way to fend off the inevitable consequences of sin—spiritual death, temptation, separation from God, and needless shame, regret, and pain. We might not be able to take the chaos out of the world, but we can experience rest in our hearts, letting Christ free us from our sin and shower us with refreshment.

Lord, before I act, help me see the ugly truth about sin: it grieves You and causes ruin. Speak to me in the quiet of the Sabbath, forgive me, and help me turn away from sin and toward Your righteous rest.

Forty-Five

REST IN CONTENTMENT

Do everything without complaining and arguing.
—PHILIPPIANS 2:14 NLT

L et's admit it: we all enjoy a good whine now and then. We complain about the weather, the long wait at the grocery store, the tough teacher at school, and how fast the grass grows between mowings. Just about anything can be turned into a complaint. As cathartic as it can feel, grumbling and complaining fall into the category of "acceptable" sins, like envy and gossip—the kind that so many of us commit that we don't think much about them.

That cathartic feeling lasts only a little while, though, and the truth is, there are no "acceptable" sins where God is concerned. John MacArthur says that complaining or grumbling "is an emotional rejection of God's providence, will and circumstances for one's life."[6] Whoa! I certainly don't consider my grumbling a rejection of God's will for my life. But at the core, complaining is telling God you don't like His plans and you know a better way—*yours.*

Complaining robs us of our rest with God. It indulges our "if only" bent. *If only my husband were more thoughtful . . . If only my child weren't so strong-willed . . . If only I lived in a bigger house. . . .* Rest is hard to come by when we choose to remain restless, waiting for better circumstances before we can be happy.

The apostle Paul used his unfavorable circumstances as a springboard toward learning to trust God. "For I have learned to be content whatever the circumstances. I know what it is to be in need, and I know what it is to have plenty. I have learned the secret of being content in any and every situation, whether well fed or hungry, whether living in plenty or in want. I can do all this through him who gives me strength" (Philippians 4:11–13). So the next time you're tempted to complain, take it as a cue: lift your circumstances to God and ask for His wisdom. Ask for a thankful heart to replace a complaining heart, and experience freedom that results in rest.

Lord, teach me to be like Paul, who learned how to be content in every situation, good or bad. Help me look at every circumstance as an opportunity to learn to trust You. Then I will be able to rest, no matter what is going on in my life.

Forty-Six

DISENTANGLED

Let us throw off everything that hinders and the
sin that so easily entangles. And let us run with
perseverance the race marked out for us.
—HEBREWS 12:1

Ever try to take a sweatpants shortcut when you're in the gym locker room? That is, to leave on your gym shoes to save time and then try to put on a pair of sweatpants? Inevitably, the sweats get tangled up and it takes twice as long to get the pants on. And every minute you spend twisted up in a knot on the locker-room bench is a minute you can't spend on the treadmill.

Entanglements work the same way. They prevent us from moving forward until we manage to calm down, take off what's holding us back, and break free. If life is a race and Jesus the Course-Setter, then sin is the great entangler. Our Enemy strategically puts obstacles in our way to throw us off course, away from God's kingdom.

One of our most common entanglements is busyness. It keeps us from quiet reflection before the Lord. It keeps us from spending restful time in His presence, evaluating our lives to identify sin. If we aren't aware of our sin, we won't feel a need to confess it, forfeiting the cleansing power God provides to set us free. Pretty soon our sin becomes a habit—so normal that we don't spot it in our day-to-day rush.

Slow down. Let out your breath. Rest a moment and take off the gym shoes that keep your pants bunched around your knees. Throw off the sin that entangles, and identify any encumbrances weighing you down in running your race for the Lord. Don't be embarrassed to ask the Lord to reveal your blind spots; we all have them.

Restful time with Him will help you avoid common entanglements, such as fear of what others think; lack of confidence in God's promises; seeking to control your life (or the lives of others); idols that you put ahead of God; lack of forgiveness toward yourself or others; perfectionism; sexual impurity; seeking security in sources other than God, and so many more. Those are things we don't need holding us back. Before you can run, and invite God to lovingly detangle your life.

Lord, I know it grieves You to watch me struggle under the weight of sin when You have the power to take away the burden. Help me bring my sins to You and unload them every day.

Forty-Seven

WELCOMED HOME

"But while he was still a long way off, his father saw him and was filled with compassion for him; he ran to his son, threw his arms around him and kissed him."

—LUKE 15:20

I've messed up everything. I don't know how I can show my face. I'll just have to take the consequences and live with the humiliation. . . . One can imagine how the prodigal son must have felt on his way back home: Dejected. Ashamed. Painfully aware of the just punishment for his mistakes.

The story in Luke tells us that the brash young man demanded his inheritance before his father was in the grave, left home, and squandered every cent. He returned home, broken and starving, realizing that he deserved no better than to be treated as a family servant. The son valued his independence and freedom more than honoring his father. Look where it got him. What a hard lesson.

Many of us feel the familiar ache of guilt, shame, and self-loathing that result from rebelling against God. These feelings often keep us from returning to the Father. We can't forgive ourselves, so we can't fathom that God would. The truth is that He is standing with open arms waiting to welcome us if we will only turn back to Him.

Notice how the prodigal son's father saw him when he was still a long way off. Rather than disowning his son, the father was waiting eagerly, watching and hoping for the son's return. Instead of giving him a cold shoulder, the father ran to his son, enfolded him in a giant bear hug, kissed him, and ordered the servants to prepare a lavish feast in celebration of his return.

If you are stuck in your sin, struggling to believe God wants to completely forgive you, know that your heavenly Father also is waiting and watching for your return. There is nothing He wants more than to restore your relationship with Him. Instead of waiting with punishment, He is waiting to celebrate your return and enfold you in His embrace.

You don't have to clean yourself up or get your act together before coming to Christ. He'll do that for you. Come just as you are, and He will make you clean.

Lord, sometimes I can't believe You could ever forgive me. You want me to dwell with You in rest and peace, but I can't until You free me from my prison of shame so I can return home. I'm ready to be released. Please come and set me free.

Forty-Eight

FIND MORE LIGHT

I have the desire to do what is good, but I cannot carry
it out. For I do not do the good I want to do, but the
evil I do not want to do—this I keep on doing.
—ROMANS 7:18–19

Have you ever stubbed your toe on the bed frame on your way back from the bathroom in the middle of the night? Or maybe you have tripped on the stairs going down into your dark basement? I hate when I knock over a cup of water on my nightstand when I'm groping to find my glasses so I can check out a noise in the middle of the night. We can't see well in darkness and risk hurting ourselves or things around us. Our sins send us into darkness too. Like Paul, we know the good we ought to do—and sincerely desire to do what is good—but can easily stumble and fall into darkness when we give in to sin's strong pull.

My mentor and Bible study author Barbara Mouser sums up our battle with sin this way: "Light obeyed brings more light. Light rejected brings the night." We need to obey the truth we know. When we do, God reveals Himself more to us, and we draw near Him in the circle of His protection and rest. If we choose to ignore the truth we know, however, we will grope around in the darkness of sin, unable to rest until we turn back to Him.

Thankfully, God has given us everything we need to find and obey the light. Christ defeated the power of sin, so those who believe are no longer under its power. In other words, we are no longer slaves forced to do what sin tells us; we have power through God to stand against sin and choose what is right. The moment we turn from our sins and trust Christ for salvation, we receive the Holy Spirit. The Holy Spirit makes us aware of sin and provides supernatural power to give us victory over it. Having the Holy Spirit means we do not have to stay locked in a tug-of-war with sin.

Be encouraged: "You are not controlled by your sinful nature. You are controlled by the Spirit if you have the Spirit of God living in you" (Romans 8:9 NLT). "The mind governed by the Spirit is life and peace" (Romans 8:6). We experience peace here and now, in spite of our sinful nature, as we submit to the Spirit's control. We can set aside the worry of stumbling and falling into the darkness of sin because the Holy Spirit helps us to obey and remain in the light. That's a truth we can rest in.

Lord, tune my ears to Your Holy Spirit so when He whispers "This is the way," I will listen and go in the right direction. When I walk in the light of obedience, I can rest knowing that I won't stumble and fall.

Forty-Nine

THROUGH HIM

We are more than conquerors through him who loved us.
—ROMANS 8:37

Self-improvement is big business. Who doesn't want to improve? We hope to become fitter, healthier, wiser, and more loving. We want to be more successful in business and more present in our daily lives. We try so hard to be good. The question is, *how good is good enough?*

Most of us end up exhausting ourselves in the quest for ever-elusive "balance." But many self-help gurus hide the hard truth that we will never attain it on our own. Today's verse reveals the key: we are more than conquerors *through Him* who loved us. The victory over sin—and all our other weaknesses—is through Christ.

The Christian life is not a self-improvement course, so you can stop trying to be good enough and rest. Jesus has done all the work for you. He offers to take every scrap of your sin, put it on Himself, take the penalty you deserve, and give you His righteousness in return. If you have received His gift of salvation, when God looks at you He sees Christ's perfection—period. Your failures were pardoned at the cross.

You must admit, the offer of salvation He holds out is too good to pass up!

Once you receive Christ's righteousness, you are invited to live in rest and freedom. If guilt or shame arises, just remind yourself Jesus has already declared you "not guilty." You do not need to pay again for your sins, which Jesus already paid for once and for all. Just turn from them and toward Him.

When temptations and trials come, know that you can overwhelmingly conquer *through Him.* When you feel weak or unable to move forward, you can continue *through Him.* Jesus said, "My grace is sufficient for you, for my power is made perfect in weakness." So like Paul we can "boast all the more gladly about [our] weaknesses, so that Christ's power may rest on [us]" (2 Corinthians 12:9). How's that for self-improvement?

Lord, I try everything to avoid being weak. But I don't want to miss out on experiencing Your power at work in me when I have reached the limit of my sufficiency. Weak people need You. I desperately need You. I can't be a conqueror without You.

107

Fifty

ARMED FOR REST

*Put on the full armor of God, so that you can take your
stand against the devil's schemes. For our struggle is not
against flesh and blood, but against the rulers, against
the authorities, against the powers of this dark world and
against the spiritual forces of evil in the heavenly realms.*
—EPHESIANS 6:11–12

One summer I was baffled by strange-looking cone-topped weeds that mysteriously appeared under a shade tree on the north side of my house. I never found them anywhere else in the yard but, even after I pulled them out, I would find more had sprung up the next day. Armed for battle, I snipped off the tops of the plants and sped off to the garden center to get some answers. It turned out they were a fungus that developed when I overwatered that area of the yard.

Our battle with sin is like my battle against the fungus. We can focus so much on pulling out the weeds of sin that we don't see the true source behind them: the Enemy and forces of evil in the heavenly realms. For victory over sin, we need to attack the underlying spiritual cause not just our behavior. Thankfully, God arms us with powerful spiritual weapons so we can succeed.

God stocked our spiritual arsenal with the belt of truth, the breastplate of righteousness, the shoes of the gospel of peace, the shield of faith, the helmet of salvation, and the "sword of the Spirit, which is the word of God." Then we are encouraged to "pray in the Spirit on all occasions with all kinds of prayers and requests" (Ephesians 6:17–18).

What a list of weapons! Our heads are protected from doubt by the helmet of salvation, which reminds us we belong to Christ. The breastplate of righteousness guards our hearts from feelings of shame and condemnation. The belt of truth joins all the pieces together as we move forward to fulfill God's plans, which include sharing the gospel of peace. And the shield of faith repels every fiery arrow that Satan launches our way. Don't think we are stuck playing only defense. We also have the sword of God's Word, packed with power and promises to force the Enemy to retreat.

Best of all is our secret weapon: prayer. Time with God renews us to return to battle and work the chinks out of our armor, and it arms us with strength. If you need a rest from your battle, enter the sanctuary of His prayer room today.

Lord, You arm me with all the weapons I need in my battle against sin. Help me to remember to use them every day, especially Your secret weapon of prayer. I am made strong when I rest in quiet prayer with You.

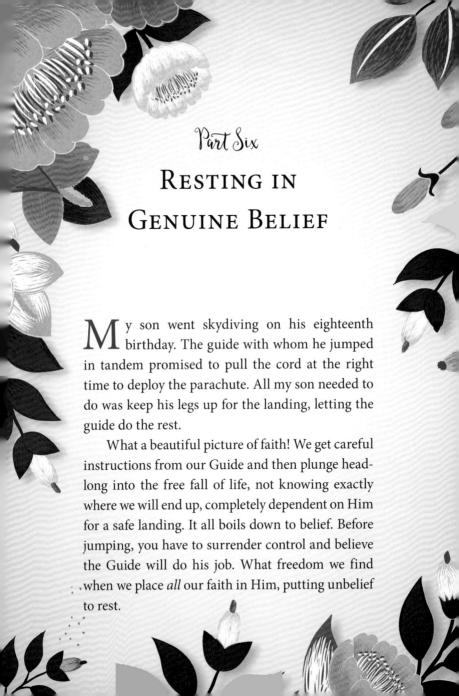

Part Six

RESTING IN GENUINE BELIEF

My son went skydiving on his eighteenth birthday. The guide with whom he jumped in tandem promised to pull the cord at the right time to deploy the parachute. All my son needed to do was keep his legs up for the landing, letting the guide do the rest.

What a beautiful picture of faith! We get careful instructions from our Guide and then plunge head-long into the free fall of life, not knowing exactly where we will end up, completely dependent on Him for a safe landing. It all boils down to belief. Before jumping, you have to surrender control and believe the Guide will do his job. What freedom we find when we place *all* our faith in Him, putting unbelief to rest.

Fifty-One

FAITH OR FEAR?

*They gave Moses this account: "We went into the land
to which you sent us, and it does flow with milk and
honey! . . . But the people who live there are powerful,
and the cities are fortified and very large. . . . We can't
attack those people; they are stronger than we are."*

—NUMBERS 13:27–28, 31

The people of Israel faced a great test of their faith. When they were on the brink of entering the Promised Land, Moses sent twelve spies ahead to assess the situation. Upon returning from their forty-day tour, they gave a glowing report about the lushness of the land and confirmed that it would be amazing to live there. But there was a problem: the natives appeared impossible to defeat. A dispute ensued between ten spies who said it was an disastrous venture and demanded they return to Egypt and two spies who said they should go up and take the land immediately and believe God would give them victory as He promised.

The ten spies looked at their circumstances and concluded the road ahead was uncrossable, while the two spies looked at God, who had promised to give them the land. The Israelites' situation showcases the great challenge of the Christian faith: taking God at His word and believing Him to do the impossible or looking at our circumstances and retreating in fear. Remember, God promised to bring the Israelites into the Promised Land, where they would dwell with Him in rest. Just as they needed faith to enter His rest, we need faith to enter His rest too.

God's rest is too precious to let unbelief cause us to miss out. His rest is a sanctuary from the busyness of life and worries that often fill our hearts. The Israelites who succumbed to unbelief missed entering the Promised Land and relishing its incredible blessings. As for the two who had been willing to move forward in faith, God led them into the land of rest along with a new generation. It doesn't make sense to say we believe God but at the same time abandon all His promises and run away in fear when the going gets tough. Anchoring ourselves by trusting in our mighty, unmovable God will keep us steady. His promises of rest are greater than our fear.

Lord, I know just how the Israelites felt when they saw the fortified cities and giants in the land. I face fear of the unknown too. Help me cling to Your ironclad promises and look to You in trust, even if the situation seems overwhelming.

Fifty-Two

FROM THE HEAD
TO THE HEART

"What is impossible with man is possible with God."
—LUKE 18:27

W hat's the difference between knowing and believing? Some call it the distance between the head and the heart. We *know* about God's promises—about His love for us, His ability to do the impossible. But how can we rest in real, deep belief in those promises?

The answer may not be hearing more sermons or reading more books about God's promises. Many of us do weekly Bible studies and hear His Word taught from the pulpit every Sunday. Our problem is acting in faith, secure in the fact that He will do exactly what He has said. For example, God promises in all things He "works for the good of those who love him" (Romans 8:28), so we choose not to give in to despair when bad things happen. Instead, we believe God's power to bring good out of the situation. Next time your mind is plagued with worry and you don't know what to do, try clinging to the following promise: "If any of you lacks wisdom, you should ask God . . . and it will be given to you" (James 1:5). If we really believe that, we'll avoid hand-wringing and have confidence that God will show us what to do.

Unbelief sets us up for a tug-of-war in our hearts, pitting our desire to walk by faith against our need for control. Wanting to control everything is one of the greatest hurdles to trusting God. When we choose belief over unbelief, we turn the reins of control over to Him. This is difficult because we often can't see from our human perspective how God could possibly work things out to keep His promises. Our human reason says, *Impossible.* But He says, "No word from God will ever fail" (Luke 1:37).

So let's stop grasping for control and open our hands by faith to receive God's rest. When troubling thoughts arise, calm your mind by reflecting on His promises. Think about them over and over until they make the journey from your head to your heart.

Lord, I have heard so much about Your promises. I have committed many of them to memory in my mind, but they seem to slip in and out of my heart. Give me grace to believe what You have promised me, to stake my very life on Your coming through, even when my human eyes can't see how.

Fifty-Three

A NEW KNOWING

"Your ancestors tested and tried me, though for forty years they saw what I did. That is why I was angry with that generation; I said, 'Their hearts are always going astray, and they have not known my ways.'"

—HEBREWS 3:9–10

Forty years should be enough time to get to know someone. Still, after all God had done miraculously to rescue His people and provide for every one of their needs, they failed to trust Him. He had proven Himself faithful and powerful, yet they did not *know* His ways.

In today's verse the Greek word for *know* is *ginosko*, which means "to come to know." It is also used as a Jewish idiom for sexual intercourse, the most intimate way two people can connect with each other. How is it possible for us to know about God and what He does but fail to know Him intimately in our hearts?

We all know who the queen of England is, but we don't know her ways—whether she is a night owl or an early riser; whether she's kind or demanding; whether she prefers clotted cream or lemon curd on her scones. We don't have a personal relationship with her.

The same can be true in our relationship with God. We can be familiar with who God is and what He does but keep Him an arm's length away. He longs to draw near—for us to invite Him to take up full residence in our hearts. If we don't, and we forego cultivating a close relationship with Him, we will find it difficult to trust Him in the big tests of life. You can't trust someone you don't know.

God clearly revealed His personal love and care to the Israelites, guiding them by a pillar of fire and cloud, feeding them bread from heaven, and parting the Red Sea so they could escape Egypt. He reveals Himself to us too, not only through every word written to us in Bible but also the ways He has personally worked in each one of our lives.

To enter into Sabbath rest, take a moment to go back and remember prayers He's answered. Call to mind ways He has worked on your behalf. I bet you'll find that the evidence of God's care in the past is overwhelming. Let's avoid the Israelites' mistake and get to know Him intimately through the Bible and all He's done for us. Then we can rest, believing that He will take care of us the same way in the future.

Lord, You have never, ever given me any reason to doubt You. I invite You to take up permanent residence in every corner of my heart. The better I know You, the more I will trust You.

Fifty-Four

SOFT HEART

Today, if you hear his voice, do not harden your hearts.
—HEBREWS 3:15

The heart is central to physical life. It pumps life-sustaining blood through the body. Without a beating heart, no mammal or human could live. In the same way, the heart, or soul, is central to our spiritual lives. Without a heart of complete trust in God, faith cannot survive. That's why Scripture issues a warning to each one of us: "Above all else, guard your heart, for everything you do flows from it" (Proverbs 4:23). A heart of faith supplies vitality to our spiritual life.

On the other hand, a heart hardened by unbelief chokes off spiritual life. The writer of Hebrews reminds us of how the Israelites refused to go in and conquer the Promised Land after a poor report from the spies. Their example warns us about the danger of letting unbelief grow. Bouts of unbelief are something all Christians naturally deal with after initial belief in Christ leads to salvation. We can't lose that salvation. But a hard, unbelieving heart can bring our spiritual growth to a standstill.

We harden our hearts when we don't act on what

we know to be true about God, His commands, or His promises. Lack of confidence in God is unbelief. Lack of confidence is why we usually don't take God at His word and move forward in faith. I don't like to think of my lack of trust in God as rebellion, but that's what it is. In my doubt, I'm really saying that God doesn't know what He's doing, so I'm going to go my way instead of His way.

Let's not take matters into our own hands. When we do, we will find ourselves mired in confusion, doubt, turmoil, and self-deceit—all hallmarks of unbelief. How do we deal with a hard heart? We'll talk about several antidotes in the days to come, but the first thing we can do is ask God to do heart surgery. In humility, we ask God to soften our hearts and renew our faith. The Great Physician promises, "I will give them an undivided heart and put a new spirit in them; I will remove from them their heart of stone and give them a heart of flesh. Then they will follow my decrees and be careful to keep my laws. They will be my people, and I will be their God" (Ezekiel 11:19–20). A heart of flesh—one that beats for Him—is a heart at rest.

Lord, a hard heart can't beat for You. I want my heart to beat in unison with Yours, and I want to hear Your voice. Help me in my unbelief and keep me near You, resting in the truth of Your Word.

119

Fifty-Five

REST TOGETHER

*Encourage one another daily, as long as it is called
"Today," so that none of you may be hardened by sin's
deceitfulness. We have come to share in Christ, if indeed
we hold our original conviction firmly to the very end.*

—HEBREWS 3:13–14

The Christian life is not meant to be a solo endeavor. Every believer is designed to be part of the church, to participate fully in a local body of believers that is a part of the universal church. God designed the church as a place where, among other things, believers could learn about God, worship, get equipped to serve, build relationships with other believers, and receive encouragement in living lives of faith.

Encouragement from fellow believers is another antidote for a hardened heart. Sometimes merely watching God work in someone else's life can inspire you to trust Him in your own. When circumstances arise that rattle your faith, another believer can remind you of God's promises and encourage You to take Him at His word. We are relational creatures, and we learn from one another. Sharing personal experiences about how God helped you overcome unbelief can keep another person from going down the same path.

There's a reason we go to church on the Sabbath. We can refresh one another with encouragement, and we can remind one another of what Hebrews calls "our original conviction"—that is, our salvation. Participating in a church body will provide a constant reminder of what Christ has done for you with His work on the cross. There's nothing more powerful than going back to the cross of Christ to strengthen you to continue believing when doubts press in. We are to hold firmly—to grasp like a lifeline—our original belief in Jesus Christ and keep holding on for dear life until the end.

For faith-filled living we constantly must return to the cross where our spiritual journey began. All our questions about God, His character, and His love for us are answered at the cross too. We can rest in the fact that we are forgiven and are loved unconditionally by Christ. If He loved us enough to die for us, then surely He will continue to be near and help us to the end.

Father, help me always to remember how much You love me. Show me how to encourage others with that love. Since You have paid the steep price of Your Son's life so I could belong to You, I can rest assured that You will never abandon me or my brothers and sisters in Your church.

Fifty-Six

THE BEST COMBINATION

While the promise of entering his rest still stands, let us fear lest any of you should seem to have failed to reach it. For good news came to us just as to them, but the message they heard did not benefit them, because they were not [combined] by faith with those who listened.
—HEBREWS 4:1–2 ESV

If you baked a chocolate cake, you wouldn't throw a few eggs, flour, sugar, cocoa powder, butter, and vanilla in a bowl and put it in the oven without mixing the ingredients together first. The cake wouldn't turn out. Instead, you would blend all the ingredients until they were so thoroughly combined that you couldn't distinguish one ingredient from another.

The same is true for our Christian lives. God's Word provides many varied ingredients, and we are to add faith—our complete trust that God will do what He says He will do. The writer of Hebrews issued a sad warning about those who did not combine faith with hearing the gospel: they fell short of the promise of entering God's rest. Faith was the missing ingredient that made true, godly rest possible.

So let's give ample attention to all the ingredients of faithful rest in God. First, the Bible: we take God's Word, turning it upside down, inside out, reading it, pondering it, memorizing it, and reminding ourselves of it until it becomes part of us. Then we combine what we read in God's Word with complete trust until both are so integrated in our hearts that one can't be separated from the other.

When we combine God's truth, we experience stability. Otherwise we will not be able to enter God's rest if we don't believe what He says. We will be subject to our emotions, riding a roller coaster of exhilarating highs when things are going well and plummeting to the depths when the unexpected intrudes. Faith is refusing to get on an emotional roller coaster and instead standing firmly with our feet planted on the immovable foundation of God's Word.

It's all about faith. Faith is the one ingredient that brings everything together. With faith touching every part of our lives, we will be able to taste the riches of walking closely with the Lord and feast on His Word. We can rest, knowing our deepest longings and needs will be met in Him.

Lord, during the darkest times in my life, Your Word has spoken comfort to me. I treasure Your words. They are like food sustaining my spiritual life, and I can't live without them. Help me combine them with faith so I can experience Your rest.

Fifty-Seven

TRUSTING REST

*Faith is confidence in what we hope for and
assurance about what we do not see.*
—HEBREWS 11:1

With technology at our fingertips, we can google anything we want, anytime, to get the facts. We can check whether our flight is on time before leaving for the airport, see if something is in stock at our favorite store, and check the menu at a local restaurant to ensure they are serving what we want before leaving the house. Normally we are uncomfortable moving forward until we have all the facts, but that's what faith requires us to do.

One dictionary defines *faith* as a "strong belief or trust in someone or something; firm belief in something for which there is no tangible proof." Having no tangible proof is what makes faith hard. But God designed it that way: faith requires trust. Faith calls us to move forward even in the face of impending disaster, failure, and unknowns, trusting God will take care of it all—especially when we do not understand exactly how He will do it. "We live by faith, not by sight" (2 Corinthians 5:7).

When living by faith, we will not be able to see the final

outcome before taking action, but we can cling to God, who is willing and able to take care of whatever lies ahead. Exercising faith can bring tremendous peace as we entrust the future to God. Wrestling with unbelief and giving up control, on the other hand, makes it hard to get there. We can't wait to act until we have all our ducks in a row. Faith asks us to move forward without all the answers.

While the requirements of faith are great, the rewards are beyond compare. Faith unlocks God's power. When we are willing to go on an adventure without googling, planning, booking, and checking, we never know what God will bring about. He can do what we could never accomplish on our own, and we experience His power at work in our lives. Best of all, He gets all the glory.

Exercising full faith is the difference between a small, controlled, ordinary life—limited to what we feel we can accomplish in our own strength—or an extraordinary life surrendered to God to use as He sees fit. Who wouldn't want that kind of life? We can rest our researching, planning minds and let God take us somewhere we could never imagine.

Lord, adventure is thrilling, but at times the unknowns also make me afraid. There's no greater freedom than when I free-fall by faith. It makes me want to trust You all the more. Every day help me put my hand in Yours and go on a faith journey wherever You lead me.

Fifty-Eight

BELIEVING IN MIRACLES

Against all hope, Abraham in hope believed and so became the father of many nations. . . . Without weakening in his faith, he faced the fact that his body was as good as dead—since he was about a hundred years old—and that Sarah's womb was also dead. Yet he did not waver through unbelief regarding the promise of God, but was strengthened in his faith and gave glory to God.

—ROMANS 4:18–20

At the time I was diagnosed with a sarcoma, a rare cancer of the soft tissue, the situation seemed impossible. The tumor was nestled in my brachial plexus, the control center for nerves that operate the arm and hand. At best, doctors thought I would have limited arm/hand function after radiating and removing the tumor. Worst case, they might have to remove my arm. With no medical tests capable of showing the full picture, doctors and I had to wait until surgery to find out.

I was ecstatic to wake up from surgery and see that my arm was still there. After conducting a successful nerve test, my normally quiet, reserved doctor literally jumped up and down at my bedside and shouted: "It's a miracle! It's a miracle!" Aside from a little residual swelling that causes me to wear a compression sleeve, my arm functions perfectly well. When people ask why I wear the sleeve, I tell them this story of God's miracle—what He did when I prayed for Him to save me from the sarcoma and spare my arm. He made the impossible happen.

God made a glorious miracle happen for Abraham too. He and Sarah waited more than twenty years for God to fulfill His promise to give them a child. Even though having a child at that point was impossible, Abraham *still* believed God. His belief gave God glory. What extraordinary faith!

We all live with the tension between the reality of our circumstances and God's power to overcome them. We give glory to God when we continue to trust Him even when all evidence is to the contrary. Glorifying God in this way gives us rest, a break from a mind swirling with doubt. When we glorify God through trusting faith, He infuses our weak, tired souls with new strength.

If impossible circumstances are rocking your world today, go to God and rest. Ask Him to give you new faith, the kind that will glorify Him and restore peace to your worried mind. Lift your voice and celebrate what Your almighty God can do on your behalf. Rest in His glory!

> *Lord, You can do all things. I give You glory today, delighting in what You can do, looking forward to what You will do, and resting patiently while You surprise me with how You will work things out.*

Fifty-Nine

"I Do Believe!"

"But if you can do anything, take pity on us and help us."
"'If you can'?" said Jesus. "Everything is possible for one
who believes." Immediately the boy's father exclaimed,
"I do believe; help me overcome my unbelief!"

—MARK 9:22–24

I do believe; help me overcome my unbelief!" This is one of the rawest and most honest statements in Scripture—and one we can all identify with. It comes from a story about Jesus and about us. The father stood in a no-man's-land between faith and doubt. On one hand, he knew Jesus was capable of doing what he requested—of driving out the demon from his son that the disciples couldn't budge. But since past attempts had failed, he doubted. He didn't want to get his hopes up. It might be too good to be true.

This kind of thinking robs us of rest. It leads to lying awake at night, anxiously wondering if the Lord will intervene on our behalf. I know, because I have stood in that no-man's-land many times. It's a torturous place, and one where unbelief grows and thrives. Still, the father in the story had a modicum of faith that Jesus could help his son.

Otherwise he would not have bothered to bring him in the first place.

Notice how compassionately Jesus led the father from a no-man's-land to a place of belief and rest. He didn't rebuke him but rather asked a rhetorical question. In effect Jesus was saying, "What do you mean, 'Can You'? I am God. Of course I can! I have complete power over everything." Then Jesus reminded the father of an ironclad truth: nothing is impossible for one who believes. Even if all other attempts have failed, belief unleashes the power of God and provides hope for the future in a way nothing else can. Belief is a shelter of rest in which to take cover from the barrage of our doubts.

One of the best prayers we can pray to put our doubts to rest is: "I do believe; help me overcome my unbelief." God doesn't require a saintlike level of faith before He will act. We can begin with our mustard-seed-sized faith and cry out to Him to remove the unbelief; then peace can come. Jesus never condemns a small faith that fiercely lays hold of Him and won't let go. He can work with that. Just ask in faith, and He will bring you to restful hope in Him.

Lord, I marvel at Your lovingkindness and compassion. You understand my weakness and know I am merely human. Thank You for taking my hand in Yours when I raise it in faith (even if it is miniscule faith) and for leading me from my place of doubt to belief.

Sixty

WORTH THE EFFORT

*There remains, then, a Sabbath-rest for the people of God;
for anyone who enters God's rest also rests from their
works, just as God did from his. Let us, therefore, make
every effort to enter that rest, so that no one will perish
by following [the Israelites'] example of disobedience.*
—HEBREWS 4:9–11

I n our hectic world, spiritual rest is hard to come by. So
we are commanded to make every effort to attain it. It
sounds like an oxymoron, but it takes work to enter His
rest! Another translation of this verse uses the word "strive"
(ESV). We are to strive—literally, to make haste—to enter
His rest. The writer of Hebrews is sounding a warning like a
tornado siren. He is imploring us to stop what we are doing
and take cover. We are in danger of being swept away with
the busyness of the world and forfeiting the rest that comes
from reliance on God's promises and full surrender to His
will. God does not want us to go through life in a state of
constant, hectic rush when we can experience the rest of
genuine faith in Him.

We are all in danger of falling into disobedience and
lack of confidence in God, just as the Israelites did when

they wandered in the desert. In today's verse the verb used for entering God's rest is in the imperfect tense. To enter God's rest is an ongoing, uncompleted action referring to a continuing or repeated event.

Each day we are to carve out a quiet space—a Sabbath moment when we stop our work and our struggling and turn intentionally to God. We "make every effort" by purposefully establishing habits that help us do this, such as getting up a little earlier and reading the Bible with morning coffee or turning off the radio and spending time in prayer on the way to or from work. Or maybe you would rather take a walk to let your mind and body unwind from the stress of the day and think about Him. Whatever you do, it means designating times without phones, technology, or noise so you have the quietness you need to recalibrate your life to God's pace instead of to the world's. "Every effort" looks like guarded, treasured, daily rest and Sabbath moments. These are gifts from God, a spiritual safeguard against being led to fall away from the living God (Hebrews 3:12). We can stop working, even if it takes a little effort!

Lord, maintaining a close walk with You requires a concerted effort. I long for the peace and rest You provide in this crazy, mixed-up world. Help me make every effort to enter Your rest every single day. It will be worth it.

Part Seven

ABIDING IN HIS PRESENCE

My sister recently gave me a Pilates bench she ordered because of an infomercial. The tutorial DVD talked about engaging your "powerhouse," those core muscles that provide stability. Core stability reigns supreme in Pilates, and you can't do the exercises successfully without it.

The same principle applies to our spiritual lives. We need a strong spiritual core or we will lack power in all the activities of daily living. We gain core spiritual strength by disentangling from daily demands to spend time alone with God. Rest with God is like engaging our "spiritual powerhouse." It stabilizes us so we won't trip and fall as we go through the taxing exercises of life.

Sixty-One

AN EXTRAORDINARY VISIT

[Abraham] was sitting at the entrance to his tent in the heat of the day. Abraham looked up and saw three men standing nearby. When he saw them, he hurried from the entrance of his tent to meet them and bowed low to the ground.

—GENESIS 18:1–2

On an ordinary day, Abraham was sitting by his tent when an extraordinary visitor came to call along with two other men. Abraham sensed the momentous nature of the occasion and hurried to greet them. He bowed as if in the presence of royalty and invited them to sit and rest while he rushed off to prepare a feast fit for a king. As Abraham later found out, the visitor was indeed a king—the King of kings.

When I was new to Bible study, I thought Jesus first came on the scene when He was born of the Virgin Mary. I had not realized that Jesus was and is eternal. He has no beginning and no end—like God the Father and the Holy Spirit. Before Jesus was born as a human to dwell among us, He appeared several times in the Old Testament. The preincarnate (before becoming a man) Christ visited Abraham.

Notice how He came in the heat of the day, a time when it was too hot for Abraham to work. Because Abraham wasn't busily scurrying about, he looked up and noticed the visitors. The Lord comes to call for us every day too. If we are too engaged in the hustle and bustle of daily life, we can easily miss His visit. Even if we recognize that He is waiting for us to stop what we are doing to meet with Him, we often delay and make that extra phone call, put one more load of laundry in the washer, or get distracted by a hundred other inconsequential things. What are these things in comparison to meeting with the Lord of the universe?

If I'm honest, I'll admit I can get so distracted that I put God off until I fall into bed exhausted at the end of the day. At that point I can barely manage to stay awake while I read the Bible and pray. We can take a lesson from Abraham, who purposely stopped working to sit down during the day. He was ready to run immediately to meet the Lord and bow down, acknowledging the great honor of the visit. If we are serious about experiencing God's rest, let's do likewise and make time to retreat from our activities so we are available to spend time with Him.

Lord, sometimes I feel as if I can't spare the time to sit and rest because I won't get everything done. But there's nothing more important for me to do than meet with You. Show me when to stop, and help me to slow down so I am available when You come to call.

135

Sixty-Two

COOL REFRESHMENT

Let a little water be brought, and then you may all
wash your feet and rest under this tree. Let me get you
something to eat, so you can be refreshed and then go on
your way—now that you have come to your servant.
—GENESIS 18:4–5

There's nothing more refreshing than the cool shade of a tree after spending hours in the hot sun. Add to that an ice-cold drink, and you have a little taste of heaven on earth. That's the kind of refreshment Abraham wanted to offer his visitors—an escape from the oppressive heat so they could be rejuvenated before continuing their journey. He brought them water to wash after many hours of walking on dirt roads and offered them a place to relax in the shade while he prepared a meal. Ultimately God wants to provide the same for us—a break from our taxing journey through life so we can be refreshed to continue on our way.

Notice what Abraham's visitors did before their meal: they washed up. In the same way, before drawing near to rest with God, we must rinse off spiritually. This means washing away all the dirt we pick up along our journey in life—the equivalent of confessing our sins, repenting, and asking

Jesus to make us clean. "If we confess our sins, he is faithful and just and will forgive us our sins and purify us from all unrighteousness" (1 John 1:9). This is not an intimidating process; it's cleansing and purifying. When we open up with a desire to remove anything that separates us from God, Jesus does the dirty work and makes us "white as snow" (Isaiah 1:18).

Once the barrier of our sins is removed, we can draw near the Lord and rest with Him. God desires to provide shelter, like a shade tree, from the scorching sun under which we work while fulfilling the various responsibilities in our lives. He holds out His branches as an open invitation to come in from the heat and rest a while with Him. The meaning of the word "rest" (*Sha`an*) in today's verse is to lean on, support, trust in, or refresh oneself through fellowship. When we rest in the Lord, we are, in effect, leaning with our full weight against Him, trusting Him to hold us up, just as we would kick back and recline against the sturdy trunk of a shade tree. Transferring our weight to the Lord, we get a well-needed break from carrying everything on our own.

Lord, how I long to rest with You when I've been burning the candle at both ends. You offer a kind of refreshment that I can't find anywhere else. Remind me to wash the dust of sin from my feet, accepting the gift of Jesus' cleansing, healing water. I don't want anything to stand in the way of drawing near You.

Sixty-Three

SABBATH NOURISHMENT

Abraham hurried into the tent to Sarah. "Quick,"
he said, "get three seahs of the finest flour and
knead it and bake some bread." Then he ran to the
herd and selected a choice, tender calf and gave
it to a servant, who hurried to prepare it.

—GENESIS 18:6–7

Abraham shifted into high-gear hospitality mode for the unexpected visitors. No expense was spared to provide a lavish feast. His visitors were worthy of red-carpet treatment. A lavish feast should be involved in our rest too. As Abraham invited his visitors, God invites us to stop, rest, and be nourished by providing us a special meal. He knows how spiritually weak we can become when all we do is grab quick snacks instead of sitting down for a full dinner.

Jesus said, "Man shall not live on bread alone, but on every word that comes from the mouth of God" (Matthew 4:4). God spreads a lavish feast for us in His Word. Why would we settle for grabbing only a fast-food meal as we hurry by? Bible study with the TV on or with music blaring in the background, pushing it aside occasionally to check for texts or the latest social media update just can't sustain us in the long run.

Jesus also told His disciples that he had another kind of food that they had yet to learn about. "My food . . . is to do the will of him who sent me and to finish his work" (John 4:34). A balanced spiritual diet consists of taking in the Word of God and then living out what we learn. If we only consume—that is, keep taking in the Word and doing Bible study after Bible study but failing to help nourish others— we'll become spiritually flabby and lethargic. If we *go-go-go* without nourishing ourselves on the Word, we'll become spiritually thin, frail, and exhausted.

It makes no sense to go through life hungry or thirsty when Jesus spreads a feast before us. "I am the bread of life. Whoever comes to me will never go hungry, and whoever believes in me will never be thirsty" (John 6:35). Jesus is waiting patiently for us to stop what we are doing and pull aside to meet with Him. He is waiting with a feast to renew us, just as Abraham spread a feast for his guests. He has nourishment full of wisdom, peace, strength, and love if we'll stop long enough to join Him at His table.

Lord, You promise if I come to You that I will never be hungry—for peace, for wisdom, for acceptance, for love. You provide everything I need. Help me to come to You and rest instead of filling up on things that don't leave me satisfied.

Sixty-Four

TAKE SOME TIME

He has made everything beautiful in its time.
—ECCLESIASTES 3:11

My daughter and I enjoy watching the Oscars and the Grammys. But we are not as interested in seeing who gets what award as we are in what the women are wearing. Watching the regal procession of ball-gowned women is like watching a modern-day Cinderella dream—except for one actress who had a nightmare moment. In her haste to get to the podium, she tripped on her beautiful gown and fell in front of millions of viewers.

The fall immediately reminded me of something my Bible Study Fellowship teacher Nancy Tyler told me years ago: "Rush is wrong." Those words often ring in my ears when I am tempted to plow forward and take matters into my own hands. The Bible is laden with examples of people who rushed forward instead of waiting for God, such as Sarah, who offered her maidservant to Abraham when she tired of waiting for God to provide a son. Or Rebekah, who schemed with Jacob to steal his brother's birthright when they feared God wouldn't bring it about. Rushing didn't end well for them. When we rush forward because we are tired of waiting for God, things never seem to end well for us either.

God's timetables often do not line up with our own. As we learn to rest, let's respect the power of time. It takes time to consult God about a major decision, to discern His will, and to make a wise choice. It takes time to let our swirling thoughts settle down so we can listen to what God has to say. It takes time to read His Word and mull it over. It takes time to talk to God in prayer. It takes time to uncover our faults and to figure out how to move forward a better way. It takes time for God to mold us into the people He wants us to become.

We receive precious encouragement and gain much-needed wisdom when we rest and make time for Him—to sit, to listen, to be present. We also save ourselves from the heartache that inevitably results when we rush to take matters into our own hands instead of waiting for God to make everything beautiful in *His time*. There are no shortcuts to developing a deep and abiding relationship with God. Let's resist the urge to rush. Let's give Him all the time He needs to weave everything in our lives together in a beautiful way.

Lord, You are never in a hurry. You take all the time You need to bring about what's best for me. You have a beautiful plan for my life. Help me to rest while You bring it about.

Sixty-Five

THE WEDDING FEAST

*Then the angel said to me, "Write this: Blessed are those
who are invited to the wedding supper of the Lamb!"*
—REVELATION 19:9

T he big day is almost here. The bride and groom have
planned for months. Now family and friends are
gathered for the rehearsal dinner. The bridesmaids and
groomsmen have received their instructions, and the couple
have practiced their vows. It's not the real thing yet, but soon
everyone will join to celebrate the couple's lifelong commitment. What joy there will be on the wedding day!

This life is like a dress rehearsal for the ultimate wedding
feast in heaven, where the Lamb of God (Jesus Christ) cele-
brates His marriage to His bride, the church. Much of what
we do in our Christian lives is intended to prepare us for that
glorious celebration. In fact, every time we pull away from
the busyness of the world to rest in the presence of God, we
are practicing what we will be doing in heaven forever.

The challenge is keeping it fresh. An engaged couple has
only one rehearsal and then the wedding. We are rehearsing for heaven every day through Bible reading and prayer,
church services, and Bible studies. These can become empty

rituals if we lose sight of the beautiful heavenly celebration they help prepare us for one day.

Let's breathe some fresh life into our rest rehearsal. When you pull aside from your everyday tasks to spend time with the Lord, remember He is the Lover of your soul. When you worship Him in your heart or join a chorus of praise at church, remember the music joins with the angels' voices in heaven. Your prayers transport you to the very throne room of God. Ask Him to help you to "see" Him in your rest rituals instead of being distracted by a million other things, such as what the person in the pew in front of you is wearing or making a mental list of things you need from the grocery store.

Remember, our spiritual vitality doesn't come from how many church services we attend, how many ways we serve, or how many prayers we say. Our spiritual life springs from *knowing intimately* the God who gave us life and wants us to be eternally joined to Him. Let's not get so busy doing things *for* God that we miss out on *knowing* God, the whole point of spiritual practices in the first place. Then we will be free to focus on the true Center of our celebration.

Lord, keep me from just going through the motions.
When I rest, I want to celebrate You and the fact
that I can experience a little heaven on Earth as I
quietly wait for the ultimate heavenly wedding.

143

Sixty-Six

THE NOURISHING VINE

"I am the vine; you are the branches. Whoever
abides in me and I in him, he it is that bears much
fruit, for apart from me you can do nothing."
—JOHN 15:5 ESV

I magine a beautiful vineyard with rows of lush green stretching miles over gentle hills. The old, twisted vines are trained onto trellises, where each spring they sprout their leafy branches and bear fruit. To stay alive, those branches depend completely on the vine, the roots of which go deep into the soil, to transport water and life-sustaining nutrients to all parts of the plant. When the vine provides the perfect balance of nutrients and moisture, the branches will thrive and produce abundant fruit. If a branch is cut off from the vine, however, it will survive only a few days before shriveling up and dying.

Our spiritual connection to Christ, our Vine, is absolutely essential for a life that will yield anything valuable or eternal. Christ supplies the spiritual strength and sustenance for our faith. Things like the cares of the world, busyness, or insistence on following our own plans can choke off His life-giving supply, leaving our spiritual lives shriveled and dry.

How do we stay connected? Today's verse says the key is abiding—a mutual abiding of Christ in us and of us in Christ. *Abide* means to stay, remain, continue to be present, not to depart. A plant must remain where the gardener places it. If the ground becomes dry, the plant can't move to a new location next to a stream. It must remain where it is. That's what God wants us to do: remain still and stay focused on Him. For us to abide in Christ, we must stay in His presence, no matter what the world throws at us to entice us away.

Through Sabbath rest, we learn to abide. We stop what we are doing, connect with Jesus, and stay with Him through every moment of the day. There's a vast difference between this and glancing over the Bible, mumbling a few prayers, and running off without Jesus into the activities of the day. As we abide, we invite His Word and the calm of spending time in His presence to permeate every fiber of our being. Staying in His presence becomes a nourishing connection to the wellspring of life when we slow down and enter His presence. This feeling of calm rest can remain with us on even the most hectic days.

Lord, help me to stay connected to You, like a branch to a vine.
I want to be attuned to You so that no matter where I go or
what I encounter today, I will maintain a steady confidence
that we are in it together and You will guide me through.

Sixty-Seven

PLANTED TO GROW

*The fruit of the Spirit is love, joy, peace, patience,
kindness, goodness, faithfulness, gentleness, self-
control; against such things there is no law.*
—GALATIANS 5:22–23 ESV

Every spring I take the little, undeveloped impatiens plants from their flat and plant them in my garden. As I set them in the ground, I hope they will grow into a vibrant wall of color to greet guests as they come to my front door. When a farmer plants seeds in his field, he hopes they will grow and produce a plentiful harvest. The whole point of planting things, whether in a pot on your deck or across acres of farmland, is to produce results—what we call *fruit*.

When we first trust Christ, He plants His Holy Spirit within us because He wants us to grow and bear fruit. God desires to produce intangible spiritual fruit—the kind that grows on the inside. Cultivating this kind of fruit can be a challenge because the rewards are not financial, material, or seen by the world. But internal spiritual growth is incredibly important. It produces character, depth, and an undergirding strength to walk sure-footed through the minefield of our mixed-up world.

Fruit produced by the Spirit includes the character qualities of love, joy, peace, patience, kindness, goodness, faithfulness, gentleness, and self-control. These are born when we put down our roots in Christ—staying in His presence, soaking up His Word, praying, learning about who God is, and becoming more like Him by spending time with Him.

What fruits of the Spirit are springing up in the garden of your life? The last time I checked mine, I found the weeds of worry, stress, and a quick temper choking out the love, joy, and peace that were trying to grow. My time abiding with Christ was wanting, and remarkably, that corresponded directly to the lack of fruit I was bearing and lack of rest I was getting.

A life that looks like a beautiful flower bed won't be possible without being well watered by a steady stream of rest. When we make time to soak up the blessings of being in God's presence, we become like Him and spiritual fruit begins to grow.

Lord, make my life a thriving, vibrant garden that brings beauty to the world around me. I want people to see You in me. Give me courage to leave lesser pursuits so I can come to You and let You change me from the inside out.

Sixty-Eight

A PRUNED LIFE

"I am the true vine, and my Father is the gardener.
He cuts off every branch in me that bears no
fruit, while every branch that does bear fruit he
prunes so that it will be even more fruitful."
—JOHN 15:1–2

I f we're honest, we admit that our lives often resemble an overgrown jungle more than a meticulously pruned topiary. It's easy to buy into the world's lie that busy is better. We tend to base our core value on how much work we do, and we feel good about our day only if we've managed to check multiple items off our to-do list. *No* is a word we avoid using at all costs. When we manage to say it, we often feel guilty because we believe worthy people can always find a way to fit one more thing into their schedules. In God's eyes, though, a truly fruitful life is a pruned life.

What is pruning? It's *deliberately* streamlining your life to remove everything that detracts from doing the most important things. A choice is involved. We must decide whom we are serving. We could choose to live for success and honor in the world's eyes, which means we must play by the world's rules of drive, ambition, and productivity—letting life grow into a jungle. Or we could decide to live for success and honor in God's eyes, which means we must play by His rules of balancing work and rest, and prune everything that prevents us from slowing down to cultivate closeness to Him.

We can't have it all. To have more of God is to have less of the world. So a pruned life will look vastly different from everyone else's life. In Kevin DeYoung's book *Crazy Busy*, he says that in addition to setting priorities, we must set *posteriorities*—"things that should be at the end (posterior) of our to-do list. These are the things we decide *not* to do for the sake of doing the things we ought to do. Making goals is not enough. We must establish what tasks and troubles we will not tackle at all."[7]

Whoa! Isn't that a novel concept—purposely leaving some things undone? It sounds freeing but it can be painful to let go of things we love. But remember who holds the pruning shears: our loving Father. And remember why He is using them. He doesn't want us to live bland, mediocre lives when we can be used to bear fruit that will last for eternity. As the all-wise God who never makes mistakes, He knows exactly what to prune so we will be laden with fruit.

Lord, bring into my life and take out what You see fit. I want my life to count more than I want to be comfortable. I want to bloom.

Sixty-Nine

REST IN THE TRUTH

Whatever is true, whatever is noble, whatever
is right, whatever is pure, whatever is lovely,
whatever is admirable—if anything is excellent
or praiseworthy—think about such things.
—PHILIPPIANS 4:8

My friend is an avid bird-watcher. She visits a bird sanctuary near her home every chance she gets. The birds are protected there from hunters and other natural predators. She enjoys the quiet stillness of her hobby and being able to see species she wouldn't be able to see anywhere else. We all need to find places like the bird sanctuary to escape the noise of our culture. God provides just the sanctuary we need: His truth.

I don't know about you, but I often feel bombarded by confusion and noise. We hear spin from PR machines, dubious claims on the Internet and social media, and relativist assurance that everybody's right, even when they conflict. Where can we find peace? Thank heaven that no matter what is going on in our lives, good or bad, we can turn to God and take shelter in the sanctuary of His truth. In a world where truth is often twisted to support one agenda or another, it is refreshing to turn to God's inerrant, unchangeable Word. It will stand forever, and we know we can trust it.

Taking sanctuary in God's Word protects us from the confusion and deception the world throws our way. The Bible shifts our focus from earthly thoughts to the things of God—things that are right, pure, lovely, and admirable. The more these thoughts rest in our minds, the less room there is for worry, confusion, and half truths. Resting our minds by thinking of godly things also transports us from our fallen world momentarily so we can experience a small taste of heaven while we are still on Earth. What a welcome break!

The sanctuary of God's truth also provides protection from a merciless predator: Satan, who is "the father of lies" (John 8:44). Knowing what's true makes identifying a lie so much easier. We don't have to hand-wring about what's right and what's wrong because God's truth clearly shows us the way.

When we need to get away from it all, let's go to the sanctuary of God's truth. In the quietness of His protection, we can take shelter, rest, and be still.

Lord, You are the Author of truth. Take me under Your wing, and teach me how to listen to You instead of to all the world's noise. Help me rest in Your truth.

Seventy

MOMENTS OF SOLITUDE

Be still before the LORD and wait patiently for him.
—PSALM 37:7

Rest comes in many shapes and sizes, just as people do. Just as God made us physically different, He also knit us together internally with unique temperaments. Some of us are go-getters, and some of us are laid-back. Some of us recharge our batteries by being with people, and some of us like to do that alone. Although we are all different, we have one common need: learning to be still.

I joke with my family that I like to multitask, so I rest while I run! My favorite time to be still and abide with the Lord is when I am running. Often I run immediately after reading the Bible. There's no phone, no children to interrupt, no media, and no undone house chores staring me in the face. I am alone in nature, in silence broken only by the rhythmic pattern of my breathing and feet striking the pavement. I think about the great honor I have to come into God's presence and how unworthy I am. Recalling my failings, I ask for forgiveness, thanking Jesus for suffering to take away my sins. I can't help but rejoice that I can experience the presence of God and His holiness in a sinful world. If I am weighed down, I will unload a heavy heart and pray about special needs for myself or others. But mostly I will think back on the Bible verses that I read and mull over them before God. Then I will ask God as if He were running alongside, "What do You want to say to me?" I remain quiet and listen, sometimes for most of the run. These listening times have been some of the most fulfilling in my Christian experience.

Abiding with Christ doesn't mean we lock ourselves away behind closed doors like monks in a monastery, investing hours a day in quiet meditation. Abiding means we recognize that our relationship with God is so critical to our spiritual well-being that we push aside the world for intentional moments of solitude to meet with Him. This can be done in as many different ways as there are people in the world. God has given me running as a way to abide with Him because it fits with the way He has wired me. He will give you a means to abide that fits perfectly with your personality too. Just remember that abiding doesn't come to an end once we have met with God. After resting in His presence, we always bring Him with us as we move back into the demands of the day.

Lord, I marvel at Your creativity and how You have shaped rest into something that can stretch to fit any size. Help me put on Your stillness today and remain in it the entire day.

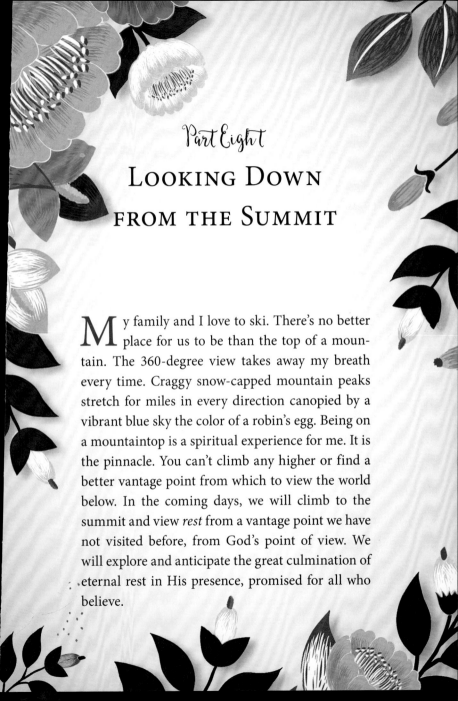

Part Eight

LOOKING DOWN FROM THE SUMMIT

My family and I love to ski. There's no better place for us to be than the top of a mountain. The 360-degree view takes away my breath every time. Craggy snow-capped mountain peaks stretch for miles in every direction canopied by a vibrant blue sky the color of a robin's egg. Being on a mountaintop is a spiritual experience for me. It is the pinnacle. You can't climb any higher or find a better vantage point from which to view the world below. In the coming days, we will climb to the summit and view *rest* from a vantage point we have not visited before, from God's point of view. We will explore and anticipate the great culmination of eternal rest in His presence, promised for all who believe.

Seventy-One

HIDDEN NO MORE

The man and his wife heard the sound of the LORD God
as he was walking in the garden in the cool of the day, and
they hid from the LORD God among the trees of the garden.
—GENESIS 3:8

We see God in His grandeur in the first few chapters of the Bible, commanding the universe into existence by the power of His words. On the other hand, we see Him personally involved in every minute detail of creating human life. From high to low, top to bottom, everything in God's creative process drove toward a relationship between Him and the people He made. But then Satan entered the idyllic garden to tear everything apart.

Most of us have heard the story of how Satan tempted Eve to eat from the forbidden tree and Adam ate too. Sin and death invaded Adam and Eve's world just as God had warned would happen if they chose to disobey Him. Their relationship was broken. All was ruined. God in his holiness could no longer dwell with them in the beautiful setting He created for that purpose.

The story could end there, but it is only the beginning. As God set out the consequences Adam and Eve would suffer because of their sin, He also held out a kernel of hope that one day He would send a Savior to defeat Satan and sin once and for all. With the creation of the world behind Him, God conducted a great rescue operation. He would save humanity from sin and restore our relationship with Him. Christ's redemptive work makes living happily ever after possible.

We do not have to hide from God. Our "happily ever after" includes the removal of all sin and God dwelling among His people in a perfect new heaven and new earth for all eternity. Hard to imagine, isn't it . . . what the world would be like without any sin? Heaven is a place of perfect rest, where God settles down to make a permanent home with the people He loves. When the going gets tough, we can look forward to this complete, eternal rest one day when all our striving on this earth will be done.

Lord, I see You differently when I look at the Bible as Your love story. I am forever grateful that You didn't give up on us when Adam and Eve sinned but put into effect a great rescue operation. Although I have tried to hide from You because of my shame and sin, thank You for pursuing me when I was running in the opposite direction. Thank You for offering me true rest.

Seventy-Two

LED TO FREEDOM

By day the LORD went ahead of them in a pillar of cloud to guide them on their way and by night in a pillar of fire to give them light, so that they could travel by day or night.
—EXODUS 13:21

Rescues don't get more dramatic than this: The ten plagues of Egypt. The parting of the Red Sea. The bread from heaven and water from rocks. All of it was the culmination of God's promise four centuries earlier to make Abraham into a great nation—Israel. Once the Israelites were freed, God immediately manifested His presence among them by leading the lost people forward in a characteristically dramatic way: as a pillar of cloud by day and a pillar of fire by night. For the first time, God's people could see with their own eyes His presence among them in the cloud and fire.

What a comfort the Israelites must have taken in God's presence leading them. They had known only the land of their slavery, where they'd been held in bondage for more than four hundred years. They had no idea where they were headed, but they knew God was with them. He intended to take them to a land where they would dwell with Him. How personally God cared for them. How powerfully He worked on their behalf.

God does the same today. He desires to set us free from our slavery—to sin, to our schedules, to materialism, to success, and to a host of other oppressors—so He can guide us safely through life to our final heavenly destination. And He will stay in front of us to lead the way.

Scripture tells us the pillar *never* left its place in front of God's people (Exodus 13:22). Although we don't have a visible column of fire or cloud to guide us, God still makes His constant presence known today through the inspired words of the Bible and in the magnificent creation around us. His teaching and guidance are readily accessible, in books or even electronically.

God still leads us out of our bondage too, though perhaps in less outwardly dramatic ways. But His rescue is just as real and just as powerful. So when He prompts us to follow Him, in big ways and in small ways, let's not allow an overbooked schedule to stand in our way. He wants to free us from the bondage of busyness so we can enter into His rest and safety. He's got a plan for us to reach the Promised Land. Will we make time to go?

> *Lord, I can be so blind to Your presence right in front of me. Please help me notice all the ways You speak to me and lead me. Thank You for rescuing me from the things that keep me from Your holy rest!*

Seventy-Three

SOME ASSEMBLY REQUIRED

*Then the cloud covered the tent of meeting, and
the glory of the LORD filled the tabernacle.*
—EXODUS 40:34

Think of the last instruction manual you read. Scintillating, right? Even if you like putting together your latest purchase from IKEA or assembling your kids' play sets, the manual usually goes in the drawer (or in the trash!) rather than on the coffee table for some light reading later.

It's tedious to read through the elaborate instructions God gave for building the tabernacle—and then read them *again* as the Bible records the construction of every element. The book of Leviticus follows, outlining the smallest details of the priesthood, sacrificial system, and a myriad of rules instructing Israel in holy living. Why all the fuss? Because God was coming to dwell.

Think about all the fuss we make when guests are coming to stay the weekend. We want everything just so. We might even rush to IKEA and buy a nightstand to assemble for the guest bedroom! But imagine if God Himself were coming, not just for a visit but to stay—permanently. We couldn't make our homes nice enough or worthy of Him, even if we spent years constructing a new house from custom blueprints. When God was about to live among the Israelites, everything had to be perfect—because God is holy.

After the Israelites finished carefully constructing the tabernacle—a portable, tentlike structure—God's presence came to dwell there. This was a monumental event. God's glory radiated in such grandeur that it could not be missed.

What a jaw-dropping, incomprehensible thought, that a holy God would want to live among a small, ragtag nation of former slaves. These were ordinary imperfect people, yet God singled them out to shower His love and blessing upon them. Through them, God would display His glory to all the nations.

God's presence rested with Israel in the tabernacle. And His presence rests in our lives too—when we are made holy. Fortunately, the complex, wordy instruction manual for making us into a holy dwelling has been drastically simplified: "If you declare with your mouth, 'Jesus is Lord,' and believe in your heart that God raised him from the dead, you will be saved" (Romans 10:9). Jesus does the heavy lifting, making us into holy dwelling places where God can be present with us.

God, it took so long for me to see that Christ is the only bridge back to You. I sat in church every Sunday but missed the point. You don't want to merely be part of my life. You want to be at the very control center dwelling within.

Seventy-Four

A HOUSE OF REST

"You will have a son who will be a man of peace and rest, and I will give him rest from all his enemies on every side. His name will be Solomon, and I will grant Israel peace and quiet during his reign."
—1 CHRONICLES 22:9

What do you imagine when you think of peace and quiet? A comfortable bungalow with books and cushions? A beachside hut with the sound of ocean waves? The porch of a cabin, nestled in the freshness of the forest? What sort of refreshment might you experience after time spent there?

Rest and peace allowed Solomon to be extremely productive during his reign. Without wartime interruptions, David's son had time to ponder the meaning of life. He became renowned for his wisdom and authored some of the best Wisdom Literature of the Bible. On top of that, Solomon constructed many glorious buildings, ushering in a golden age for Israel. By far his crowning achievement was building a temple for God—"a house as a place of rest" (1 Chronicles 28:2)—so that God's presence would no longer be confined to a tent. Solomon fulfilled his father's dream of making a permanent residence for God. In his dedicatory prayer, Solomon said, "Now arise, Lord God, and come to your resting place, you and the ark of your might" (2 Chronicles 6:41). There the people would worship, and God would show His glory in spectacular ways.

These restful times were something like a mountaintop experience for Solomon. He had a unique opportunity to focus on God, which flowed out in blessing to those around him. When we follow Solomon's lead and create places of rest, God can do amazing things in us too. At the summit, we can be inspired to serve Him in ways our cluttered minds couldn't see when we were down in the valley of the everyday. We need open space free from the squeeze of life's pressures to ponder who He is, why He has put us here, and how we should live.

In quiet moments, whether they're restful retreats or time reserved during an ordinary day, let yourself be refreshed by the mountain air of God's inspiration. When you do, your heart will become a "house of rest" for His Spirit, rather than a container for the cares of the world.

Lord, help me construct places of rest in my day, making room for You to meet with me and inspire me. When I come down from the mountaintop of Your presence, help me to bring what you have shown me to a needy world below.

Seventy-Five

A HEART THAT
WELCOMES GOD

"Where is the house that you will build Me? And where is the
place of My rest? . . . But on this one will I look: on him who is
poor and of a contrite spirit, and who trembles at My word."
—ISAIAH 66:1–2 NKJV

Yes, Solomon's temple was unbelievably lavish and the Israelites' tabernacle was built to perfection. But neither of these buildings could truly contain God. Why? Solomon said, "The heavens, even the highest heavens, cannot contain you. How much less this temple I have built!" (2 Chronicles 6:18). As the Creator of all things, God has the universe as His dwelling place. But He desires to be intimately close to us, so close that He is looking for hearts to dwell in—hearts fully devoted to Him.

While Solomon's temple looked amazing on the outside, the hearts of the people were becoming crumbling ruins where God couldn't rest. The book of 2 Chronicles tells us that they began going through the motions when they brought their sacrifices. Their actions at the temple were correct, but their love of God had turned stone cold.

God looks straight into our hearts. Delighting in the things of the world can begin to fill our hearts, leaving less and less room for Him to dwell in, along with His rest and peace. Pretty soon the little things that distract us from God turn into big things, and before we know it, the peace of the Lord has departed.

That's what happened to the Israelites. Their compromises led to a pattern of repeated rejection of God until they reached the point of no return. "The LORD . . . sent word to them through his messengers again and again, because he had pity on his people and on his dwelling place. But they mocked God's messengers, despised his words and scoffed at his prophets until the wrath of the LORD was aroused against his people and there was no remedy" (2 Chronicles 36:15–16). Eventually enemies captured Israel and turned the temple to rubble—a fitting reflection of the hearts of the people.

If your wholehearted devotion to the Lord is crumbling in places, ask Him to do His divine repair work. Ask Him to help you make room by removing devotion to worldly things so He can dwell in every corner.

Lord, You can see what no one else can see: the state of my heart. Bring me to new levels of truth and honesty about what goes on inside it. Remake my heart into a welcoming place for You.

Seventy-Six

GOD'S SOLUTION

The Word became flesh and made his dwelling among us. We have seen his glory, the glory of the one and only Son, who came from the Father, full of grace and truth.
—JOHN 1:14

Houston, we've had a problem. An *Apollo 13* astronaut transmitted this message to NASA when he realized that the space capsule was losing oxygen so quickly it would run out before the crew made it back to Earth. The world held its breath as engineers worked to find a solution to the life-or-death situation.

Those of us with our feet firmly planted on planet Earth also have a life-or-death problem: sin. And we waited centuries for God to reveal the solution. It started with Adam and Eve's ill-fated choice in the garden, passed through successive generations, and multiplied further in the Israelites. When they rejected God, His presence departed His earthly place of rest in the temple. Approximately four hundred years followed, when the voice of God was silent and men held their breath wondering when God might reveal the solution, which He had hinted at back in the garden. That glimmer of hope planted centuries earlier illuminated the earth when the

Solution arrived: Jesus Christ, "the true light that gives light to everyone was coming into the world" (John 1:9).

Mankind would no longer be stuck in the darkness. Jesus, the "light of the world" (John 8:12), would not be restricted to the temple as God's glory was in the days of Israel. Jesus would provide light for the entire earth to show all men the way back to God. And His salvation would make it possible for the Holy Spirit to dwell in an individual's heart, something infinitely better than dwelling in an earthly building, a temple. Jesus Christ, full of God's glory, came to "[make] his dwelling among us" (John 1:14).

What glorious hope this gives us for true rest and peace! The God of the universe is not just *with* us but *in* us, to dispel any shadow of darkness, sin, fear, confusion, or doubt. God shines His light on the turmoil of this world, and the darkness will never be able to overcome it, no matter how crazy and mixed-up things become. Let's rest in this truth and bask in the Light that chases away darkness.

Lord, You solved my life-or-death problem with sin, something impossible for me to do on my own. Thank You for the loving solution of Your Son—the One who turns my darkness into light.

Seventy-Seven

A PLACE TO LAY
YOUR HEAD

"Foxes have dens and birds have nests, but the
Son of Man has no place to lay his head."
—MATTHEW 8:20

Where do you lay your head? A favorite armchair worn in all the right places? A comfy couch or a fluffy pillow? Like a bird in a nest, you can snuggle into that place after a hard day and feel at ease. But Jesus didn't have such a place. He couldn't find a place of ease in our world because He doesn't belong here. The Father sent Him to Earth on an errand, to pay for the sins of the world. Jesus' job was to work so He could bring us rest—now and in the life to come.

Like us, Jesus knew firsthand about working around the clock. The demands on Him were enormous: sick to heal, masses to teach, apostles to disciple, Jews to win over, and miracles to do. It was all part of the agenda the Father had set for Him. Yet under all the pressure, Jesus never lost His equilibrium. He had no permanent nest or den, so He regularly traveled to quiet, lonely places to talk to His Father and renew His strength. Going to His Father was Jesus' rest.

With the salvation of mankind on His shoulders, Jesus clung steadfastly to His connection with God, realizing He couldn't do the job on His own. "For I have come down from heaven not to do my will but to do the will of him who sent me" (John 6:38).

God gives each of us a mission along with spiritual gifts that uniquely equip us for our work. Just as Jesus was dependent on the Father, we can't complete our work on our own either. We need a deeper rest to maintain equilibrium than a cozy armchair or a comfy couch can provide. We need the rest of our heavenly Father.

When you sink into your favorite armchair at the end of the day, remember to rest your head on the Father's shoulder too. Ask Him to renew your strength and to provide all you need to continue to do the work He's given you. In those quiet moments, ask Him to show you if you might be trying to take on extra work that goes beyond His plan. That way you can use your precious energy on the right things—the way Jesus did. And you can find true rest in the Father the way Jesus did too.

Lord, I have only one short life with which to make a difference for eternity. That job is too big for me to do on my own. When I take a break from working, remind me to renew my strength by both resting my head on my pillow and resting in You.

WELL-TIMED REST

[Jesus] said to them, "My soul is overwhelmed with sorrow
to the point of death. Stay here and keep watch with me." . . .
Then he returned to his disciples and found them sleeping.
—MATTHEW 26:38, 40

Jesus agonized in prayer in the Garden of Gethsemane.
He knew He would soon have to suffer on the cross to
pay the price for the sins of the world. His work for God
was reaching its climax. He asked His disciples to come
with Him, to stand by Him at His time of greatest need. But
while He cried out to the Father, begging Him to spare Him
but willing to go on, the disciples fell asleep. When Jesus
needed them most, they couldn't keep their eyes open.

How do we know when it's the right—or wrong—time to
rest? There are seasons in our lives for resting and regroup-
ing, and times for laboring with all our strength. I don't know
about you, but I don't want to be like the disciples and miss
out on something important God wants me to do because
I'm too exhausted or too busy doing something else. That's
why it's important to stay in tune with God. If we ask Him,
God will give us the discernment to know the difference.

Asking yourself the following questions also might

help: What am I wearing myself out on—things that really matter, or of a temporary nature? If I continue to invest my efforts the way I am now, will I have regrets in the end? Is my schedule managing me, or am I managing my schedule? Am I overwhelmed or empty most of the time, needing to give myself permission to slow down? The best part is that you don't have to figure everything out on your own. God's wisdom is available for the asking.

Even if you are in a tough place, it doesn't mean you are doing the wrong thing. As Christ demonstrates, sometimes the work God assigns isn't easy. Our work might include suffering, sacrifice, surrender, frustrations, and loneliness. God knows we are human, and He knows we need rest and reprieve from the unavoidable strains of life: "He gives strength to the weary and increases the power of the weak" (Isaiah 40:29). It costs us something to follow Christ, but the joy of an eternal reward and the opportunity to glorify Him are worth it. So seek wisdom as you work, searching for God's timing. Then you will be ready to go and ready to set aside everything and rest when He asks you.

Lord, time is short and precious. Give me wisdom to know when to seize the moment and when to rest. When You put something on my heart to do, help me to respond right away before the opportunity slips away.

Seventy-Nine

A SAFE PASSAGE

*"Behold, the ark of the covenant of the Lord of all the earth
is passing over before you into the Jordan. . . . And when the
soles of the feet of the priests bearing the ark of the LORD, the
Lord of all the earth, shall rest in the waters of the Jordan,
the waters of the Jordan shall be cut off from flowing."*
—JOSHUA 3:11, 13 ESV

One of the greatest fears in life is death. It commonly appears on the list of top-ten fears. But the Bible talks about death in a peaceful way, as falling asleep or resting.

Crossing the Jordan River is a metaphor for death in the Bible, a picture of smooth sailing from the shore of life to the other side. In today's verse, when the priests carrying the ark of the Lord stopped and rested in the Jordan river, the waters stopped flowing so God's people could cross easily on dry ground. Before they made the crossing, God instructed that the ark, representing His presence, should go first.

God sent His Son, Jesus, to go ahead of us too. Jesus makes the crossing from this life into our eternal rest an easy journey, since He blazed the trail ahead of us by triumphing over sin and death. Those who have received forgiveness of their sins do not need to fear what will be on the other side.

It will be unimaginably glorious. "No eye has seen, no ear has heard, and no mind has imagined what God has prepared for those who love him" (1 Corinthians 2:9 NLT).

Jesus assured the disciples that He would prepare a place for them in heaven. "And if I go and prepare a place for you, I will come back and take you to be with me that you also may be where I am" (John 14:3). We don't need to fear death because when the time comes, Jesus Himself personally will come to escort us to our heavenly home. We will never be alone. The moment we are "away from the body," we will be "at home with the Lord" (2 Corinthians 5:8).

Our death means a smooth arrival in the harbor of the Father's presence, an eternal safe haven. No more straining against the waves or fearing we'll lose our way in the darkness of night. When we lie down and put our head on the pillow of death, our sleep will be even sweeter than a wonderful night's rest snuggled under the covers of our own bed. We can welcome a rest like that.

Lord, thank You for making a place for me in heaven and promising to hold my hand when it's time for You to bring me there. I rejoice that I have a perfect rest to look forward to one day.

Eighty

REST IS HERE

*Let us then approach God's throne of grace with
confidence, so that we may receive mercy and
find grace to help us in our time of need.*
—HEBREWS 4:16

Yes, we'll rest in heaven. Of course that is our hope. But we also hope we don't have to leave this mortal coil in order to get some rest! Keeping our eye on the prize of heaven can get us through challenging times, but we don't have to wait to arrive there to experience heavenly rest and peace. When Jesus opened the door for us to enter heaven's rest, He meant for that sacred rest to make a difference in our everyday lives on Earth. We can go straight to God's throne room in prayer—now, while we live—to talk to Him and ask for His help whenever we need it.

In the Old Testament, the high priest was the only person able to go behind the curtain into the holiest place of the temple where God's presence dwelled—essentially His throne room. The priest could go only once a year, and never without bringing the blood of a sacrifice to pay for his and Israel's sins. When Christ died to pay for all our sins, the curtain was torn in two (Matthew 27:51). What an astounding change! We can approach the God of the universe ourselves, personally, with any need we have. Not only that, but we can do it boldly—knowing that He won't reject us, because Christ makes us holy.

The bottom line is that we are not alone. God does not stand aloof in a distant galaxy unaware of our plight. Intimately aware of every detail of our lives, He is on call 24/7 to hear our cries for help. Even when we are not praying, Jesus is always interceding for us as we make our way through life (Romans 8:34). If knowing this doesn't allow us to rest, I don't know what will! We can access God's power, strength, wisdom, comfort, and anything else we need from His overflowing storehouse of blessings whenever we need it. We don't have to wait for heaven to connect with God.

Lord, I can run to You whenever I am in trouble. I can lay my head against Your beating heart and be enfolded in Your loving arms to rest whenever I am weary or afraid. You are always there for me, even when no one understands. Thank You for sending Jesus so I can go to You anytime.

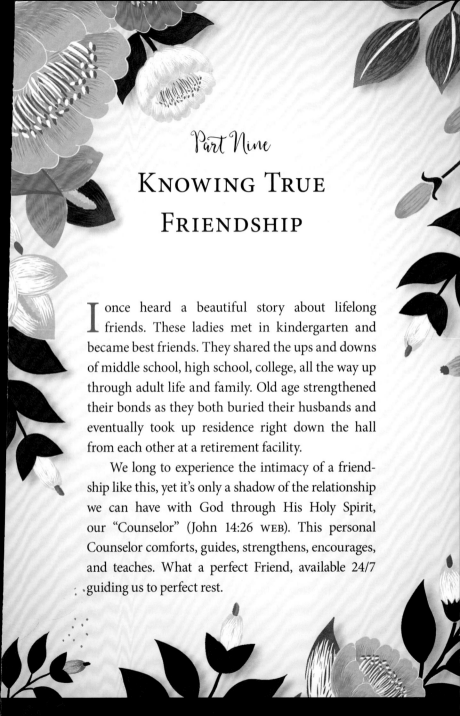

Part Nine

KNOWING TRUE
FRIENDSHIP

I once heard a beautiful story about lifelong friends. These ladies met in kindergarten and became best friends. They shared the ups and downs of middle school, high school, college, all the way up through adult life and family. Old age strengthened their bonds as they both buried their husbands and eventually took up residence right down the hall from each other at a retirement facility.

We long to experience the intimacy of a friendship like this, yet it's only a shadow of the relationship we can have with God through His Holy Spirit, our "Counselor" (John 14:26 WEB). This personal Counselor comforts, guides, strengthens, encourages, and teaches. What a perfect Friend, available 24/7 guiding us to perfect rest.

Eighty-One

A HOLY BREEZE

*Suddenly a sound like the blowing of a violent wind
came from heaven and filled the whole house where
they were sitting. They saw what seemed to be tongues
of fire that separated and came to rest on each of
them. All of them were filled with the Holy Spirit.*

—ACTS 2:2–4

All of us can appreciate a summer breeze ruffling the curtains, bringing an unseen, cooling relief inside a stuffy room. Imagine what the apostles must have experienced when they heard a violent wind filling their house—but not a curtain stirred. They must have sensed immediately that something supernatural was going on. That's when they saw what looked like flames of fire, something the Bible often uses to indicate God's presence, separating and resting on each of them. They knew the Holy Spirit was coming, but I bet none of them could have conceived His arriving the way He did. It had to have been an unforgettable experience.

Something incredible was taking place. The Holy Spirit of God came down from heaven to take up residence in individuals. He comes to rest steadfastly and immovably in the hearts of people to make His home there, never to leave. The act of the Holy Spirit resting on the disciples also marked them with a seal—a stamp of approval on their redeeming transformation.

The Holy Spirit does not take up residence in all people, only those who have been made holy by confessing their sins and professing faith in Christ. This means we can't earn our way to heaven by our own merit or doing things we think will make God happy. We can't accomplish holiness on our own. Only Christ can make us worthy of heaven and able to receive the Holy Spirit.

Have you felt the supernatural breeze of the Spirit? Has He come and brought the cooling relief of God's divine presence? There is no need to go without our personal Counselor and perfect Friend. Ask today for Him to rest on You.

Lord, the Holy Spirit is a wonderful mystery. I can't touch, feel, see, or hear the Spirit, but He is real like gravity and the oxygen I breathe. The fact that You live in me means there are endless possibilities for Your transformational power to work in me. It's always possible for me to change, and there are unlimited ways You can use me to accomplish Your purposes. You amaze me!

Eighty-Two

A LIVING TEMPLE

Do you not know that you are God's temple
and that God's Spirit dwells in you?
—1 CORINTHIANS 3:16 ESV

The Garden of Eden. The tabernacle. Solomon's temple. The body of Jesus. God has dwelled with man in many different ways over the years, showing us a beautiful picture of how He wants to be near us. Then through the Spirit, He made *us* His dwelling.

We are the building, the temple, where God's Spirit dwells. No longer will He manifest His glory to the world in a building made by men. Instead, He visits personally, first through His Son and then through us, the "containers" of His Holy Spirit. What an honor and responsibility it is to be the vessel where God's Holy Spirit dwells!

How do we become the best vessels we can be? By inviting the Spirit to be actively involved in our daily lives and removing hindrances. We are commanded not to "grieve the Holy Spirit of God" by making Him sorrowful by our sins (Ephesians 4:30). And we are not to "quench the Spirit" by going our own way, stifling His divine influence, and suppressing His power to work instead of following His lead (1 Thessalonians 5:19).

The Spirit invites us to stay in tune with Him. He desires for us to create quiet places and empty spaces in our schedules to pray and wait for His answers. God promised, "I will put my Spirit in you and move you to follow my decrees and be careful to keep my laws" (Ezekiel 36:27). When we spend restful time in the Spirit, He shows us how to apply God's laws to our everyday decisions and dilemmas. That's the secret to remaining clean vessels where the Spirit's power can work unhindered in our lives. In that way, we are the Spirit's temple. When we invite Him to fill us, He helps us display His glory, and we shine out to the lost people who need hope. Through us, the lost can learn what it means to rest in God.

> *Lord, it's unfathomable that You see me as a temple for Your Spirit. Help me display Your goodness and power. Then others can come to know You too.*

181

Eighty-Three

POWER SOURCE

*"But the Helper, the Holy Spirit, whom the Father will
send in my name, he will teach you all things, and will
bring to your remembrance all that I said to you."*
—JOHN 14:26 ESV

Would you shovel your driveway by hand if you had a
beefy snowblower sitting in your garage? Would you
trim your bushes with handheld pruning shears one branch
at a time if you could use a power trimmer? Of course not.
Unless you *wanted* to spend hours working by hand, you'd
choose to tap into the power tool every time.

Often we plod through life expending great energy in
our own efforts while ignoring the Power Source available
to us. The Father gives us the gift of the Holy Spirit to help
us live the Christian life. "But you will receive power when
the Holy Spirit comes on you," Jesus told His disciples (Acts
1:8). The Spirit plays a multifaceted role by advising, encour-
aging, comforting, strengthening, teaching, convicting of
sin, and guiding us into truth. To begin, we receive the Holy
Spirit the moment we believe as "a deposit guaranteeing
our inheritance" (Ephesians 1:14)—our place in heaven as
part of God's family. The "Spirit gives life" (John 6:63) by

regenerating our souls. And He continues His work to make us more like Christ each day, changing us from the inside out. The Holy Spirit always sees us as works in progress.

If we have the Power Source of the Holy Spirit available, what would stop us from plugging in? Sometimes we are too busy, too distracted, or even too proud of our own abilities to recognize our need. We might think we can get along fine with our handheld shears. But then the enormity of the garden catches up with us. Often we don't cry out for God's help until we have drained all our own resources. But He longs to take the little shears from our hands and give us His power instead. We don't have to do it the hard way on our own!

If you feel powerless in your life, it's not because God is holding back on you. Ask the Spirit to help you. The Holy Spirit is always available to fill us, moment by moment. As we rest, let's listen, seek God, and stay open to the Spirit's leading. Set down your tiny tools—they're impediments to His work—and enjoy the freedom that working in His power brings.

Lord, thank You for Your patience. I'll never be perfect. But with You I don't have to be. I surrender to the life-transforming work of Your Holy Spirit. Show me how to walk in Your power each day.

Eighty-Four

POWER MADE PERFECT

*He said to me, "My grace is sufficient for you, for my power
is made perfect in weakness." Therefore I will boast all the
more gladly about my weaknesses, so that Christ's power
may rest on me. . . . For when I am weak, then I am strong."*
—2 CORINTHIANS 12:9–10

Shortly after I was diagnosed with breast cancer, a woman
came up to me at church. In an attempt to encourage me she said, "Having breast cancer was one of the most
blessed times of my life." I walked away thinking, *Yeah, right.
There's no way breast cancer could ever be a blessing. Not in a
million years.* For me, cancer meant having an insidious, life-threatening invader in my body that no one could guarantee I
would defeat. Cancer gripped me with fear and would not let
go. To add salt to my wounds, I felt guilty that I couldn't see
cancer as a blessing the way my friend did.

I struggled with God for months in an attempt to find
rest until I realized what today's verse tells us. *The power of
Christ rests more on us when we are at our weakest than at
any other time.* When Christ told Paul this fact, Paul in effect
said, "Well, bring it on then, Lord! Pile on the hardships. The
weaker I am, the more of Your power You'll give me." This

makes no sense in worldly terms, where we prize strength and we try either to escape or to hide our weaknesses at all costs. Not so with God. He can't fill us with His Spirit if we are already filled with ourselves. We must empty ourselves of our own sufficiency and admit our utter helplessness before God's Spirit can work unbounded.

We can let out our breath and stop frantically clawing to survive. We can rest knowing it's not all up to us. It's up to Him. And He has an inexhaustible storehouse to draw from in meeting all our needs. That's why my friend, in her weakness, felt God's nearness and power during cancer treatments in a way she had not felt when she was healthy. When the chips are down, God works most powerfully in our lives. We can rest in weakness, because He makes us strong.

Lord, when I am broken, helpless, overwhelmed, and can't go another step, You are waiting to pick me up and carry me forward. Thank You that I never have to be afraid that I can't handle life. Your power takes over at the place where mine runs out.

Eighty-Five

OVERCOMERS

*"He who overcomes, I will grant to him to sit down
with Me on My throne, as I also overcame and
sat down with My Father on His throne."*
—REVELATION 3:21 NASB

Imagine the relief an athlete would feel after running an ultramarathon, swimming the English Channel, or climbing Mount Everest. He or she might be dirty, bloody, frostbitten, or exhausted, but none of that would matter compared to the joy of finally overcoming—and resting. The same joy awaits us when our work in this life is through. When we have persevered despite our difficulties to fulfill God's purposes, we will have the privilege of sitting down and resting with Jesus. He invites us to sit with Him at the right hand of God, where He rested when His mammoth task on Earth was finished.

Staying the course with Him will reap a joyous reward. So don't stop now. Keep going! Paul encourages us: "In all these things we are more than conquerors through him who loved us" (Romans 8:37). What an incredible promise.

Conquerors showcase God's glory. When He empowers a beaten-up, broken-down, weak human being to do His miraculous work, the world sees a glorious display of God's strength. This shows the world He's real, not some cosmic force far removed from the everyday affairs of men. And God's blessings don't stop there. Overcomers also join the exclusive, eternal fellowship of the Father, the Son, and the Holy Spirit by following their pattern of work and rest.

The Father rested after His great work of creating the world; Jesus sat down at the right hand of God and rested after accomplishing the salvation of the world; and the Holy Spirit rests upon those who believe, guiding them to their eternal home. When we arrive in heaven, we also will sit down and rest with Christ after completing the work God has given us. Plus, we will be at Jesus' side to see the grand finale when the world is judged, all evil is put away, and paradise is ushered in.

Remember, you are more than a conqueror through Him. Though you might arrive at the finish line spent, nothing can compare to the unspeakable joy of resting in your eternal reward if you persevere to the end.

Lord, heaven is going to be amazing. When the going gets tough and the Enemy tempts me to despair, remind me that the stakes are too high to drop out of the race. I want to rest at Your right hand! Help me to remember that I am more than a conqueror through You.

Eighty-Six

TRAILING DEEDS

*"Blessed are the dead who die in the Lord from
now on." "Yes," says the Spirit, "they will rest from
their labor, for their deeds will follow them."*
—REVELATION 14:13

E very time I come home, I ask my daughter, who has been
puppy-sitting, "How was Oakley?" I can count on her
answer being the same 99.9 percent of the time: "She slept the
whole time." This makes me a little mad—not because I want
Oakley to be naughty, but because I want Oakley to sleep
most of the time for me too. Instead, she follows me wherever
I go. Even if she is dozing serenely in the corner of the kitchen,
the minute I leave the room, she's at my heels. She's like a
chick following a mother hen, except that this chick weighs
more than one hundred pounds!

Just as I can't shake Oakley, our work will follow us to
heaven too. We won't be able to separate ourselves from it.
All we have done will be examined. What is eternal will be
rewarded, and what is frivolous will be burned up. What a
sobering thought. Scripture tells us, "Each one should build
with care" (1 Corinthians 3:10). And, I would add, each one
of us should spend our time with care. Our time is limited.

Our opportunity to work will come to an end when we enter the rest of death. There will be no opportunity for a redo. Therefore, we should invest ourselves in things that will not burn up in the end so we can receive our reward—including holy rest.

Notice that our deeds don't precede our arrival in heaven, but they trail along behind us. That's because our deeds don't earn our place in heaven. Christ covers us! We don't have to carry around the burden of people-pleasing or guilt anymore. We don't have to exhaust ourselves trying to control everything to ensure things turn out right. We can relax and stop worrying about whether we've done enough to get into heaven. Christ's death and resurrection provide forgiveness from our past, present, and future sins. They are *all* paid for, and we are stamped "NOT GUILTY."

So rest. Rest in His unconditional love and acceptance. You don't have to prove yourself to Him. Trade busy self-improvement for quiet time and relationship building with the God who loves you.

> *Lord, thank You that life is not all about me. It's all about You—finding You, knowing You, loving You, serving You, and glorifying You. If I live for You, I won't have to worry about having regrets.*

Eighty-Seven

OUR CHOICE

A man reaps what he sows. Whoever sows to please their flesh, from the flesh will reap destruction; whoever sows to please the Spirit, from the Spirit will reap eternal life.
—GALATIANS 6:7–8

U p can't be down. Light can't be dark. Wet can't be dry. Heaven it has its opposite too. As we rest in the hope of heaven, we cannot avoid thinking about its opposite. Everyone will spend eternity somewhere, either resting in the presence of God or forever removed from His presence to suffer torment. These are difficult truths to swallow, but that is what the Bible says.

What a stark contrast between eternal rest for believers and eternal punishment for those who reject Christ. In heaven believers will join angels surrounding God's throne, worshipping Him unceasingly. In heaven there will be no sun or moon to shine because the glory of God will give it light. Nothing impure will ever enter there. We can know *now* with 100 percent certainty where we will end up because this life is our choosing time. Once we die, our opportunity will have passed. Jesus wants you to choose Him, "that by believing you may have life in his name" (John 20:31).

Once we make that choice, Jesus can make all the difference. He doesn't want us merely to survive, but to thrive. "I came that they may have life and have it abundantly," meaning a life that is full and meaningful (John 10:10 ESV). Jesus knows that busyness, constantly striving to get ahead, amassing material wealth, and trying to get our kids on the best sports teams or into the best colleges—although not bad things—won't truly satisfy us in the end. He wants us to invest ourselves in things that will last, that will truly matter in the end, like sharing the gospel with others so they will be able to join in our eternal rest. Think about it: Would you choose busyness over being part of God's plan for someone else's eternity?

Seeds will spring up to yield eternal life. Those are the seeds we want to plant instead of letting busyness with lesser things get in the way. There's a certain comfort knowing our efforts will matter in the end. We can rest knowing that if we live with eternity in mind, it will make all the difference.

Lord, help me spend my time wisely today, planting seeds for eternity instead of living only for the here and now. Let me seize every opportunity to tell others how they can enter the joy of Your eternal rest.

Eighty-Eight

HAPPILY EVER AFTER

*He will wipe every tear from their eyes. There will
be no more death or mourning or crying or pain,
for the old order of things has passed away.*

—REVELATION 21:4

When I was young, I dreamed of the kind of love that every young girl longs for: a warrior prince who rides in on his white horse to rescue her from evil so they can live happily ever after. I dreamed of true love. With God this fairy-tale dream can come true for all of us. In the greatest love story ever told, Jesus' redemption, He defeats the enemies of sin and death in an epic battle, making a happily-ever-after ending possible.

Things have come full circle. From the Garden of Eden to God's great rescue operation at the cross, He has ardently pursued us in love so we could be reunited with Him. The final chapters of the Bible describe how all sin will be gone as God replaces the universe with a perfect new heaven and a new earth. In the end, we will dwell with God in paradise for eternity. This is our happily ever after, our eternal rest.

Jesus, our great Warrior, triumphed over Satan to save us from suffering and sin, once and for all. It's hard to imagine what a world void of sin will be like, but it is God's gift. Out of love He fought to spare us from the havoc sin wreaks in our lives so we can experience an eternity of His glory and goodness instead.

The constant driving force behind God's actions throughout the Bible is His longing for a relationship with us. He initiated it, He maintains it, He pursues His people when they go wayward. God will go to any length to make a relationship with Him possible. In fact, as mankind drifted farther and farther from Him, He pursued us with greater passion to the point of sacrificing His only Son. If you ever doubted God's love for you, you need doubt no more. Just look at what He has done for you out of His unconditional, faithful, sacrificial, passionate, and tender love. He is personally concerned with every detail of your life. He has always been engaged in a relentless pursuit to bring you to Himself. Rest in His perfect love as you look forward to heaven's happily ever after.

Lord, who would not want to respond to a love like Yours? You will wipe every tear from my eyes; only You know how many I have shed over the heartaches in my life. How I long for my happy ending, dwelling with You in perfect comfort, security, and peace.

Eighty-Nine

THE CULMINATION

He who was seated on the throne said, "I am making
everything new!" . . . He said to me: "It is done. I
am the Alpha and the Omega, the Beginning and
the End. To the thirsty I will give water without
cost from the spring of the water of life."
—REVELATION 21:5–6

Here it is, the great crescendo at the end of the symphony when all the themes come together. As individual music notes are combined to tell a symphonic story, every word of God's redemption plan is carefully composed to bring us to the moment of final redemption. From alpha (the first letter of the Greek alphabet) to omega (the last letter), God has been in complete control, sovereignly reigning over the entire universe and the everyday affairs of mankind. He is the beginning of all things as Creator of the world and the ending of all things as the final Judge who sentences sin, death, and Satan to an eternity in the lake of fire. The world is remade, and we are brought to live with Him.

"It is done" resounds across a new cosmos, echoing Christ's proclamation "It is finished" from the cross. Everything has come together.

The book of Revelation reveals only a glimpse of the awe and wonder of heaven—golden streets, streams of living water, light emanating from the Lord like the sun. We will worship Him there. Most important, *we will enter His rest.* We will live with Him in His house, where we will experience perfect satisfaction and peace. We will rest from toil, sorrow, temptation, persecution, and the ill effects of sin. All our hearts' desires and longings, which we have thirsted to fulfill in this fallen world, will be quenched by the spring of living water flowing from God's throne (Revelation 22:1–2).

Our souls were made for fellowship with Him, and we will be completely satisfied in His presence, never to be separated from Him again. Everything will be made new—new bodies, new attitudes, new environment, and a new, unhindered, face-to-face relationship with God. As you rest today, take a moment to stop and marvel. Listen to the symphony of God's overwhelming love for us, His children. Let your heart dance.

Lord, I'm so thankful that because of You, I will be made new, inside and out. I will see You in all Your glory, as You really are. Focus my heart on that time in the future when I won't have any work to do, except to let my heart overflow in adoration of You.

Ninety

MAKE ROOM

"Here I am! I stand at the door and knock. If anyone
hears my voice and opens the door, I will come in
and eat with that person, and they with me."

—REVELATION 3:20

A beautiful gold envelope hiding in the mail catches your eye. A special invitation must be inside as you see your name scrolled in beautiful calligraphy across the front. Attention to every detail goes into planning a wedding, down to the invitation. The bride carefully counts all the RSVPs to ensure not only the wedding but also the reception comes off without a hitch. Imagine a bride's horror to arrive at the reception and find there are not enough tables and chairs for her guests. No room! Not everyone will be able to sit down and eat.

Today's verse is Christ's embossed invitation for all of us to know Him intimately—to open the doors of our hearts and let Him in where He can settle down and share a fellowship meal with us. Beautifully wrapped gifts accompany this meal: not only forgiveness and salvation, but an opportunity for Him to rest with us and us to rest in Him.

But often we can't take Him up on His invitation because

there's no room. Our lives are full. Too full with activities, with material goods, with our own plans, with pleasures and recreation. Too full with self-sufficiency, anxiety, pride, and social media. Maybe we don't even make it to the door when He knocks because we are not at home. We're too busy running around. Or maybe we're so exhausted that we can't make ourselves get up and open the door so He can come in.

He's such an important Guest, how could we forget to make room for Him? We get so busy trying to keep up with the Joneses and climbing the corporate ladder that we don't realize that one day, all the Joneses' stuff will wear out, and the corporate ladder will crumble. Fellowship with Jesus reminds us that our worth is not based on what we can accomplish. Our relationship with Him is the purpose of our creation.

We've all been filled up and distracted by the cares of the world, leaving little to no room to sit and rest. Jesus wants to come in and help us rearrange so we can carve out a broad expanse for Him and His rest. No matter what state your heart and home are in, take Him up on His invitation and ask Him to come in. Give Him a permanent seat at your table, and enjoy living with Him in a rhythm of work and rest.

Lord, I invite You to rearrange the contents of my life so there is plenty of room for rest and fellowship with You, the most important Guest who will ever be on my list.

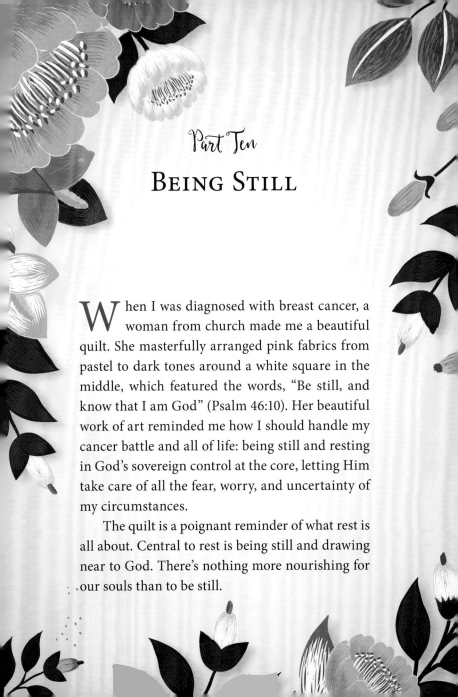

Part Ten

BEING STILL

When I was diagnosed with breast cancer, a woman from church made me a beautiful quilt. She masterfully arranged pink fabrics from pastel to dark tones around a white square in the middle, which featured the words, "Be still, and know that I am God" (Psalm 46:10). Her beautiful work of art reminded me how I should handle my cancer battle and all of life: being still and resting in God's sovereign control at the core, letting Him take care of all the fear, worry, and uncertainty of my circumstances.

The quilt is a poignant reminder of what rest is all about. Central to rest is being still and drawing near to God. There's nothing more nourishing for our souls than to be still.

Ninety-One

RECEIVE IN STILLNESS

"Be still, and know that I am God."
—PSALM 46:10

Today's verse is at the heart of my rest journey. God not only gave me a quilt with this verse on it, but He also gave me a bracelet. Think He was trying to tell me something? These words are etched in a silver cuff my sister gave me before I began chemotherapy for breast cancer. To get chemo, I had to sit still in a chair for hours while the drugs dripped one drop at a time through an IV into my bloodstream. Similarly, for radiation treatments I had to lie perfectly still while the medical team positioned me (sometimes a twenty-minute process) and stay that way until a machine finished sending beams of radiation into my tissue. To be honest, my first instinct on treatment days was to bolt from the room and run far away where the doctors could never find me. I had to force myself to be still so I could receive the lifesaving treatments I needed.

Long after treatments, I still need to force myself to be still. The bracelet reminds me to do that. Why? So I can know God. Knowing God is a spiritual lifesaving treatment I continue to need—and one we all need. To be healed from the damage of sin and to remain strong spiritually, we must regularly draw from our Power Source, God Himself. Another translation of Psalm 46:10 is: *"Cease striving* and know that I am God"* (NASB). We are to give up our struggle to find value, meaning, and significance from the things we do. We don't "bolt" and find another solution. Instead, we sit quietly. When we do, we can focus on the unseen spiritual reality that Christ values us beyond compare, even though we don't have to work at it at all. Those quiet listening times have been some of the most rewarding parts of my Christian experience. They align me with the heart of God. When God's Word doesn't match my experiences or feelings, I know that my finite understanding needs to change because His Word is always right. Quiet meditation gives God an opportunity to change my understanding—to heal me, and to eradicate any traces of the things that separate me from Him. When I look at my bracelet, the words *Be still* remind me that God's work of healing my soul is a continual, loving process. So I'll cease striving and let Him do His work.

Lord, knowing You is the greatest privilege on Earth— and the greatest challenge. I think that's why it is more fulfilling than anything in our human experience. Pry my hands away from all the worldly things I cling to, and help me be still. Tune my ears to Your voice and heal me.

Ninety-Two

QUIET WATERS

*The LORD is my shepherd; I shall not want. He
makes me lie down in green pastures. He leads
me beside still waters. He restores my soul.*
—PSALM 23:1–3 ESV

Lush green pastures blanketing the countryside, inviting us to lie down. Quiet waters bringing cool refreshment to parched souls. Restoration and renewal. What a promise for the tired and weary. Today's verse is a life-giving picture for those of us battling stress and fatigue, for those of us who feel as if there's never enough time to get everything done.

The Lord our Shepherd watches as we exhaust ourselves and wants to show us a better way. Our Shepherd knows when we have reached our limits; He knows when we are in danger; He knows when we have lost our way; He knows when we are physically hurting, weak, or exhausted. Our Shepherd also knows the geography of our lives and can lead us to green pastures and streams of refreshment so we can regroup.

Sometimes that means the Shepherd will take us to unexpected places. After a particularly demanding time in my life, I was talking to an older woman about how to recover. I felt burned-out and wanted to find the inner joy I seemed to have lost. She asked me, "What delights your soul?" I was hard-pressed to answer her because I hadn't given any thought to the state of my soul in months. I love nature and realized that I needed to make room to watch the sunset, take an occasional walk, and accept my friend's invitation to kayak anytime at her lake home. I needed to sit in my car for a few minutes when I was out running errands, look up at the clouds, close my eyes, and soak in the warmth of the sun. I also love snuggling with my daughter on the couch and listening to her talk about her day. These are such little things that make all the difference.

What delights your soul? Where would the Shepherd like to lead you for rest? Green pastures lie all around you. Even on the busiest of days, we can carve out moments to let our Shepherd lead us beside quiet waters of refreshment to restore our souls.

Lord, You don't want me to be constantly in motion; You want me to lie down in green pastures and do nothing at all. I'm so grateful that the state of my soul is of utmost importance to You. Help me value quiet moments where I can simply enjoy the world You have made.

Ninety-Three

OUR REFUGE

*Whoever dwells in the shelter of the Most High will rest
in the shadow of the Almighty. I will say of the LORD, "He
is my refuge and my fortress, my God, in whom I trust."*
—PSALM 91:1–2

Where do you live? Where are you truly at home?
Where do you feel the most comfort and protection? No matter how safe and comfortable you feel there, you probably know in your heart that it's not 100 percent secure. A curveball could come at any minute: a phone call from a doctor, a natural disaster, a random act of violence, losing a job or loved one unexpectedly, financial reversal, or any other scenario. Anything can change without notice. That's why our true refuge can't be found in a physical location or in our circumstances.

Our circumstances, however, are not beyond God's control. Taking shelter in Him is the safest, most secure place to be. If we make our home in Him, by living constantly in a state of trust, we will rest no matter what life brings. No threat can overpower Him. Nothing happens without His knowledge or permission.

He exerts more power than any force in the universe.

He can speak the world into being with one word, and He can defeat an army without any weapon by the power of His might. He can do anything on your behalf to fulfill His purposes for you. No one and nothing can defeat Him. We can rest in the shadow of His great strength that towers over us, just as we would find protection from the scorching sun by taking shelter in the shade of a majestic tree.

God is also a fortress of protection from all threats in our lives. Like a mighty wall built around us, God controls what He will allow to pass through. In His perfect wisdom, He also knows what to do about whatever comes our way. With Him as our Refuge, it's always safe to let down our guard. We can rest and set aside our worries because we can count on Him to take care of us.

> *Lord, when something rocks my world, let my first thought be of You—Most High, Almighty God. Please give me grace to trust You moment by moment every day. Help me to take refuge in You no matter what is happening in my life.*

Ninety-Four

THE LAND OF THE LIVING

*Return to your rest, my soul, for the LORD has been
good to you. For you, LORD, have delivered me from
death, my eyes from tears, my feet from stumbling, that
I may walk before the LORD in the land of the living.*
—PSALM 116:7–9

How has God been faithful to you in the past? How has He answered prayer, provided for needs, intervened in circumstances, or given guidance at a crucial crossroads? Remember these things—treasure these things. God's fulfilled promises build hope for the future and greater faith that He will act in the same way in the days to come. If there's one thing we can count on in a fallen world, it's that something will go wrong. Instead of dwelling only on challenges, however, the psalmist rejoiced in God's deliverance. He called to mind the times God heard His cry for help and intervened on his behalf. Only then could his soul be at rest and he could walk ahead in the "land of the living."

The opposite of the "land of the living" might be considered the doomsday mind-set, believing that things will never change or fearing that another disaster is waiting around the corner. It's a shadowy, draining existence. Instead, eagerly expect God to show up and bring about what is best, no matter what happens. Look for Him to act. Watch to see how He will fulfill His promises. Let this occupy your mind instead of dread or worries. "Set your minds on things above" (Colossians 3:2).

This focus is a surefire antidote to worry and fear. Our minds don't multitask. They can't simultaneously worry and trust God. Instead of exhausting ourselves by pushing fears out of the way, we can turn our eyes toward God. Our minds often dwell on things that will never happen, creating a great deal of unrest. But Jesus reminds us, "Who of you by worrying can add a single hour to your life?" (Luke 12:25). If your worries are phantoms you don't know are real, dismiss the thoughts. Remind yourself of the great works of God, and walk with Him once again in peace—in the land of the living.

Lord, I tend to forecast the worst-case scenario for the future instead of seeing You up ahead, ordering all the circumstances of my life. But You have never failed to hear my cries when I'm in need. Help me to dwell on Your faithfulness and love so earnestly that there will be no room for doubts to intrude.

Ninety-Five

THE CROSSROADS

"Stand at the crossroads and look; ask for the ancient paths, ask where the good way is, and walk in it, and you will find rest for your souls."
—JEREMIAH 6:16

Crossroads are places of decision. Robert Frost captures the dilemma in his poem "The Road Not Taken." The traveler in the poem contemplates which road to take, realizing that choosing one probably means not being able to come back to see where the other would have led. Only in looking back could Frost's traveler see how his decision worked out for him: "Two roads diverged in a wood, and I—I took the one less traveled by, And that has made all the difference."

The outcome for each road is a mystery for us. But not so for God. That's the beauty of following an omniscient God who knows all things. The crossroads never present a mystery to Him.

In today's passage, God tells His people to "look" and to "ask." He wants us to stand still for a moment and carefully consider which path we choose, asking Him for wisdom about how to proceed. Because He knows everything, He knows the good way, the best way. We need never operate in a vacuum when making decisions, because we have the ancient truth of God's Word to guide us. We have historical accounts of God's people in the Bible too, so we can learn from their mistakes and triumphs.

If you want rest for your soul, choose God's path. Initially His path might not appear to be easy, safe, or inviting. One thing is certain—we can count on God's path to be one less traveled. "For wide is the gate and broad is the road that leads to destruction, and many enter through it. But small is the gate and narrow the road that leads to life, and only a few find it" (Matthew 7:13–14). Especially where rest is concerned, this means we will be living and working in a pattern far different from the way the world operates.

Like Frost's traveler, we don't know how things will turn out. But we don't have to panic because God knows how everything will turn out. We can rest—truly rest—in a way that seems foreign to the world. That is, without worry about our path. If we're walking close to Him, we're sure to walk with peace and rest. "In all your ways submit to him, and he will make your paths straight" (Proverbs 3:6).

Lord, I confess there are times when I want to be just like those around me instead of being like You. But I don't always see at the time where that path will take me. I want to remember and walk in Your way. It's the best way. Help me stick to it.

Ninety-Six

JUST BE

"I desire steadfast love and not sacrifice, the
knowledge of God rather than burnt offerings."
—HOSEA 6:6 ESV

M y grandma Herdina always told me that God made
us to be human *beings*, not human *doings*. I knew
exactly what she meant. In her old age, with painful arthri-
tis, she moved slowly to do everything. As her world grew
smaller due to limited mobility, her understanding of life
and God grew bigger. She had time to sit and think, to watch
me and my sisters, and to pray. She saw how busy we were
studying to earn top grades, working to pay for college,
playing sports, and running around with friends. Our lives
were full.

Full lives aren't bad in themselves. But Grandma warned
us about being busy *doing* things all the time instead of
merely *being*. My life continued in a busy pattern as I eventually married, had children, and began serving at church. We
were there for every event. I even took on serving as director
of women's ministries. I prayed that God would help me not
only to do that but also to be a stellar mother and wife at the

same time. It turned out that Grandma Herdina was right. I spent so much time doing things for God that I missed knowing Him intimately.

I fell into this trap because my life was void of rest. My grandma's warning was based on Scripture—today's verse, Hosea 6:6. Later, Christ said the same thing to the Pharisees. They were so busy performing ritual obligations that they missed the point. God desires steadfast love more than sacrifices. He wants us to draw near and know Him, not merely jump through the hoops of our religious obligations.

We don't always have to look forward to our next responsibility. We can set our agendas aside and be in the moment. Just *be*. Grandma Herdina was an expert at this. One of my fondest memories is sitting at her kitchen table and drinking tea from one of her delicate china teacups with her listening to me talk as if there were nothing else more important to do. As you walk through life, ask God to show you opportunities to just be. It can provide not only a blessing of rest for you, but a blessing of presence to others.

Lord, help me stop occasionally and lift my eyes heavenward so I can focus on You. Help me to be present, to take time to enjoy the little blessings You have hidden in the world for my pleasure. Show me how to be and not just do.

211

THE IMMOVABLE ROCK

Yes, my soul, find rest in God; my hope comes from
him. Truly he is my rock and my salvation; he is my
fortress, I will not be shaken. My salvation and my honor
depend on God; he is my mighty rock, my refuge.
—PSALM 62:5–7

M y family and I love to ski in the Rocky Mountains in Colorado. We often enjoy skiing off the beaten path, through the trees on more rugged slopes. Skiing on this type of terrain is always an adventure because we don't know what we will find. Sometimes a steep turn around a mogul will reveal a rock hiding on the opposite side, immovable and often unavoidable. Many times it's too late to do anything but ski over it and hope it doesn't dig too far into the base of the ski. One thing is for sure—the rock will not move. It's up to the skier to avoid it.

God is our Rock, and He doesn't move either. His character and promises are frozen and immovable for all eternity. He never changes. We can count on Him being the same "yesterday and today and forever" (Hebrews 13:8). Not only is He unchanging, His love endures forever; He reigns forever; His plans stand firm forever; He will be exalted forever;

His Word remains. He is the only unchangeable, immutable, living God we can cling to with 100 percent certainty. If we put our hope anywhere else, we will be disappointed. Everything in our world is subject to change; but God is constant—our Rock.

Many of us have seen edifices crumble: skyscrapers, banking systems, companies, economies, maybe even relationships. Things we thought would stand like monuments forever exist no longer. It reminds us that the only place to find rest—true security—is in God. He is our Refuge, our Fortress that nothing can penetrate unless He allows it. Whatever boulders we encounter on the path will have to contend with His strength. What safety we have when we take shelter in Him!

Lord, thank You that You are my Rock and my Fortress. When I stand on You, I will not be moved. When doubts come, help me to remember that my future depends on You—that I don't have to hold everything together because You've already got it covered.

Ninety-Eight

TIME-OUT

That night the LORD appeared to him. . . . Isaac built an altar there and called on the name of the LORD.
—GENESIS 26:24–25

Isaac arrived exhausted in the town of Beersheba after a period of great difficulties. A famine had decimated His homeland. He had relocated his family twice, created problems by lying about his wife, and endured protracted feuds with local herdsmen. It must have seemed like endless trouble. Finally, when Isaac came to a place of rest, God spoke to him. God confirmed the covenant that He had made with Isaac's father, Abraham.

All of us can identify with Isaac as we run around putting out fires. We might not have to contend with obstinate herdsmen, but we do have to deal with locking keys in the car, sick children, arriving home from vacation a day late because of airport delays, washing-machine breakdowns, and more. Ugh! Life is messy. How we need a respite. When we make time to rest the way Isaac did, God can speak to us and restore our sanity. He does this through His Word, the Bible. His words can be a stabilizing force in the chaos of life.

With all we have to deal with, though, it can be challenging to find time to read and contemplate the Bible.

But we'll handle life so much better if we do. Let's take Isaac's lead in the chaos of life and put ourselves in time-out. Finding a place of solitude and silence is necessary to calm down and regain God's perspective. Usually when the upheaval of life is bearing down on us, the last thing we think to do is to find a quiet place to rest and connect with God. Our tendency is to keep engaged in the fight, which means we needlessly miss out on drawing on God's strength and help. When you feel the stress rising, fight your natural urge to plow ahead. Instead, seek a quiet time of rest with God to refocus, listen to His Word, and call on Him for help. It will make all the difference.

God, when I'm caught in a "When it rains, it pours" situation, slow me down. How I need Your Word to regain equilibrium, to remind me of Your promises, to remind me that You did not intend for me to handle life on my own. I need a time-out as an adult as much as I needed it when I was a child. Help me take it.

Ninety-Nine

OUR DELIVERER

Asa cried out . . . "LORD, it is nothing for You to help. . . . Help us, O LORD our God, for we rest on You, and in Your name we go against this multitude."
—2 CHRONICLES 14:11 NKJV

Let's face it, life can seem overwhelming at times. Sometimes we feel as Asa did, when a million men from Ethiopia and their chariots came against him to do battle: outnumbered, outgunned, and up in the air. Armies aren't coming against me, but I have piles of laundry from a family trip, a car in the shop, empty cupboards, Christmas decorations long-past due to put away, two sons to get ready to return to college, a manuscript deadline—and I have come down with a horrible head cold. I am achy, my strength is sapped, my mind is foggy, and I all I want to do is curl up in a blanket and lie down.

Asa didn't curl up in a ball and retreat when the chips were down. He went boldly to God and asked for help. He focused on God's power, remarking that it was "nothing" for God to help. Unlike us, God never grows weary. His power is perfect. Even when God does something grand, such as perform a miracle, it does not drain His energy. He is always more than adequate to help us with any task, great or small. Asa knew God could deliver him and his people, regardless of their lack of manpower or chariots. Notice how he could rest in God. *Before* asking for help, Asa focused *first* on God's power and resources. With these firmly in mind, he presented his need.

When we look to God's power and character *first* when we are overwhelmed, it can change our whole mind-set. In light of God's power, nothing is doomed to defeat. Looking to Him gives us rest from the turmoil that creeps in when circumstances feel impossible. We can pray expectantly once we remember whom we are calling on for help—our God, who easily can overcome the obstacles stacked against us. Then we can move forward in His name, resting in the promise of His strength instead of retreating in defeat.

Lord, I need You—always. I need You especially when I am overwhelmed and exhausted. I rest on You today to help me move forward, in Your name, to do what I have to do in spite of how I feel. Thank You for providing all I need.

One Hundred

THE CHALLENGE OF REST

In the heavens God has pitched a tent for the sun. It is like a bridegroom coming out of his chamber, like a champion rejoicing to run his course. It rises at one end of the heavens and makes its circuit to the other.

—PSALM 19:4–6

If there's one thing we've learned in our time together, it's that rest is not easy. In fact, learning to rest has been one of the most challenging endeavors of my life. I feel like a champion athlete whom God has had to put through strict training so I could run the course of life with the right pacing to reach the finish line. The most important part of my training has not been learning to run—that's intuitive in our accomplishment-driven society where resting feels like a waste of precious time. The most important part of my training has been learning to rest. God does not want us to miss out on the most vital aspect of our race through life: knowing Him. Rest is inextricably linked to our relationship with Him. Time invested in knowing God is as crucial to spiritual life as air and water are to physical life. That's why we were created—to know Him, not only to achieve.

He wants each of us to rejoice as we run our course like

the sun, by pacing ourselves in rhythm with Him, rising in the morning, shining brightly in the heat of midday, then settling in for an evening's rest. What a different course from the pattern of our hectic world.

Are you willing to run your course on God's pace? Are you willing to live in a rhythm of work and rest as God created you to do—even if the world is running at maximum speed? Perhaps when we make time for rest, we will have fewer accolades or awards to show for what we have done. But we will have something far more valuable. We will be trading earthly gain for the heavenly treasure of knowing God and all the blessings that go with it.

You can find rest. You were created for it. The Maker of the universe gives you rest as a gift and moves heaven and earth so you can find it for your body and your soul. It's beautiful to realize that accepting this gift is a commandment—one that's a pleasure to follow. As you go forward on your path, stay close to God, and enjoy His holy rest. Surely this will make us rejoice as we run our course.

> *Lord, thank You for the things that have made me step back and evaluate my hurried lifestyle. Help me no longer push myself well beyond the boundaries You set for work and rest. Help me make time to draw near You, the One who holds it all in His hands. Help me to be still and know You, always.*

NOTES

1. "Stressed-Out American Women Have No Time for Sleep," last modified 2007, accessed May 22, 2017, https://sleepfoundation.org /sleep-polls-data/sleep-in-america-poll/2007-women-and-sleep.

2. John Ortberg, *The Life You've Always Wanted* (Grand Rapids: Zondervan, 1997), 94.

3. Corrie ten Boom, *Clippings from My Notebook: Writings of and Sayings Collected by Corrie ten Boom* (Nashville: Thomas Nelson, 1982).

4. Hannah Whitall Smith, *The Christian's Secret of a Happy Life* (1875; repr. Nashville: B&H Publishing Group, 2017).

5. John F. MacArthur, *The MacArthur Study Bible.* (Nashville: Thomas Nelson, 2006), 1738.

6. MacArthur, *The MacArthur Study Bible*, 1718.

7. Kevin Young, *Crazy Busy* (Wheaton: Crossway, 2013), 62.

ADDITIONAL STUDY RESOURCES

Study Guide: Finding Rest . . . in a Restless World — rhythmsofrest.net